forever flowers

ANTONIA DE VERE

forever flowers

DRY

–

PRESERVE

–

DISPLAY

SCHIFFER PUBLISHING

4880 Lower Valley Road • Atglen, PA 19310

Library of Congress Control Number: 2020952427

Produced by BlueRed Press Ltd. 2021
Designed by Matt Windsor
Type set in Plantin

ISBN: 978-0-7643-6207-1
Printed in India

Published by Schiffer Publishing, Ltd.
4880 Lower Valley Road
Atglen, PA 19310
Phone: (610) 593-1777; Fax: (610) 593-2002
Email: Info@schifferbooks.com
Web: www.schifferbooks.com

For our complete selection of fine books on this and related subjects,
please visit our website at www.schifferbooks.com. You may also write
for a free catalog.

Schiffer Publishing's titles are available at special discounts for
bulk purchases for sales promotions or premiums. Special editions,
including personalized covers, corporate imprints, and excerpts, can
be created in large quantities for special needs. For more information,
contact the publisher.

We are always looking for people to write books on new and related
subjects. If you have an idea for a book, please contact us at
proposals@schifferbooks.com.

Other Schiffer Books on Related Subjects:

*Framing Floral Techniques: Floral Design Skill Building, Inspirations
& Explorations*, Renee Tucci, ISBN 978-0-7643-6200-2

*Floral Accessories: Creative Designs with Wendy Andrade, NDSF, AIFD,
FBFA*, Wendy Andrade, ISBN 978-0-7643-5446-5

For those we have loved and lost,
you are forever in our hearts.

A Note about Foraging
Foraging is collecting non-cultivated plants from the wild. The laws about foraging differ from country to country, and in the United States, from state to state. Before embarking on a foraging expedition, check your local laws and bylaws; if you are collecting from non-public land, make sure you have the permission of the landowner first.

It can be a highly contentious issue, not only from a legal point of view but also as a health issue. Many wild plants are toxic, and some can harm simply on contact. Usually a small amount of foraging for personal use only is permitted. Never collect or dig up any endangered species under any circumstances. Also, be aware that plant material is also animal food; anything you collect may be leaving wildlife hungry.

CONTENTS

1	Introduction	6
2	My Dried Flower History	8
3	My Studio	18
4	Floral Styles and My Work Process	28
	Ikebana Style	34
	Cottage	40
	Ultrapop	46
	Installations	48
5	Tools and Techniques	50
	Tools	52
	Air Drying	58
	Silica Drying	60
	Water Drying	62
	Spiraling	64
6	Dried Flower Directory	66
	Spring	68
	Summer	70
	Fall	72
	Winter	74
7	Step-by-Step Floral Pieces	86
	Posies	86
	Bouquets	100
	Ikebana Style	114
	Wreaths	128
	Circlets	144
	Hanging Pieces	162

INTRODUCTION

From an old vase with a few faded hydrangeas on the mantelpiece, to nothing short of a full-size tree floating 10 feet off the ground in a national art gallery, the past decade has seen the humble dried-flower arrangement make resurgence in popularity. Emerging out of the dusty depths of backyard shed obscurity, dried flowers have moved onto the list of must-have, in-vogue pieces, giving their fresh cousins a strong run for their long-held status as the classic go-to for florals.

Now making feature appearances in both the home and the office, dried florals can be seen in many of the world's restaurants, boutiques, and commercial office spaces. Florals now appear as anything from a softly textured bespoke arrangement, nested in a custom-made vase alongside a candle in a cosy brasserie, to a modern statement of refined, sculptural branches with scattered pockets of colored floral accents, playing off organic materials against a concrete and glass office foyer. The humble dried floral has become a staple item to dress the scenes of many home- and design-focused publications to humanize completed projects for photo shoots. And more formally, it's not uncommon to see dried floral garlands, centerpieces, or large suspended installations at events and weddings where they are used as spectacular focal points.

However, the relative ease of accessibility to dried flowers and foliage in most places is one of the most wonderful aspects of this material and means they're not relegated only to corporate settings. Many private homes also proudly display anything from a couple of loose dried stems plucked while out walking, to a delicately assembled dried arrangement, created with elements picked from just outside the front door. More often than not, these florals have been arranged by the residents or owners themselves. Today—as with the how-to journals of the1970s—you'll find an abundance of resources online simply bursting with do-it-yourself advice for the selection, drying, and assembly of dried flowers and foliage.

I have been a part of this industry for over a decade now, and from the start I have tried to nurture the revival of dried florals. From humble beginnings in a small home-studio / spare bedroom, to shipping bespoke orders internationally from a large, dedicated floral design studio, I have managed to create an extensive body of exceptional, unique, and personalized pieces that have assisted in the establishment of the dried-floral revival.

Most artists work with paint and canvas, stone and chisel, but I prefer to use nature to produce beautiful arrangements that last, and I'd like to share what I have learned with you in this book.

Left: Antonia in reflection, in her pink studio

Right: Gold and white colors give a feeling of autumnal warmth.

MY DRIED
FLOWER
HISTORY

I grew up in a lovely city: Christchurch in New Zealand, widely known as the "Garden City." It gained its nickname for the many, many, beautiful home yards, and also for its large and magical botanical gardens, which almost envelop the central city. My family frequently explored these wonderful gardens, and, with so much nature to discover, we would find a new flower every time we visited.

Our house was no exception to this civic reputation. My mother's gardens have always been beautiful and large, her personal happy place, so growing up I was constantly with her in our backyard wonderland, watching or helping as best I could. Naturally, most of my knowledge of plants, and especially flowers, was learned from her. Now into her seventies, every time I call her she is invariably in the garden.

Growing up as a "garden child," it was only to be expected that I was fascinated by the flowers and things that grew around me—I was constantly picking and eating them.

In common with many children growing up surrounded by nature, I have always been creative—I could probably make before I could talk! I taught myself many crafts and was quite artistic even from a young age. Always drawing, painting, and crafting, I was quite happy making things alone in my own little world. I was fascinated with flowers; I was always plucking them apart, sometimes drawing or painting my childish interpretation of them. At home my mother had lots of framed botanical prints, and I loved them so much that I was always trying to draw them, in wiggles and squiggles with a crayon or two.

I liked to press flowers, then set them in the recycled paper I made myself, and sold them as cards in little markets about the city. If I wasn't squishing flowers between the pages of my books of fairy tales, I would be taking rose cuttings and sprinkling them with magic dust (actually, plant hormone rooting powder that helps cuttings grow). In time, I learned how to grow new rose bushes out of these same cuttings. My mother confirmed that I was especially good at growing a particular honey-colored rose.

I have always been a bit of a hustler—my father liked to say that I could sell a car to a car salesman. I always dreamed of having a small shop of my own, or making things I could sell. My first venture (a failure), when I was seven or so, was a candy store inside my unusually large wardrobe. It had a secret room in it, an absolutely fantastic site I thought—unfortunately, no one save my mother bought my old Easter eggs or unwanted candies. I learned my lesson; a better site and customers were most definitely needed!

Right: A selection of some of my favorite dried materials—wheat, hydrangeas, poppy heads, pampas, and pea grass—waiting to be collected into an arrangement.

Below: I was a "garden child," helping my mother in the backyard whenever I could. I have her to thank for my love of flowers.

Below: Smelling roses with my father. He encouraged my interest in plants and flowers.

My school education was artistic for the most part. In elementary school right up to secondary school, my strengths were in the arts. When I found out that my high school was far too academic and didn't offer a range of arts subjects, I changed to a school where the subjects were more interesting (to me). Later, I went on to study fashion design, jewelry design, aromatherapy, and, finally, floral design. I often left my courses half finished because I wasn't interested in the full formal degree—instead, I wanted to learn what I needed, then pack up my bags and move on. I have what you might call a Gemini's curse—knowing a little about a lot.

I just wanted to soak up facts, methods, and practices that inspired me. My studies in everything might make me sound a bit flaky, but today I can see (and others have mentioned) that everything I studied—for however long—played a big part in what I create and make today. My constant search for knowledge has never really ended; I still search for enlightenment. I also met the love of my life, Mark, at design school—he later become my husband and business partner.

My most flower-related education (and the one course I actually completed) was in rather-staid floral design. I was always pushing the boundaries and asking to learn more—I was definitely not a shrinking violet. I was there to learn all I could, and often challenged my teachers. And although nothing dried was taught at my floral school (that was something I had to teach myself), I did learn a lot about flowers and the technical aspects of floristry.

While crafting and art remained my favorite pastimes, as I got a little older I also became an avid reader, mostly nonfiction and largely historically based. I was truly obsessed (and still am) with the past. My interest in ancient civilizations has become a particularly big factor in the work I create today. I was especially taken with ancient Egypt. Even from a young age I was fascinated with Egyptian treasures, its complicated mythology, and its preserving techniques. All these later inspired much of my work. As a child I knew the hieroglyphic alphabet by heart and would write code notes in hieroglyphs to my best friend—or indeed anyone, regardless of whether they understood my code. (Later in life I went on to take university papers in ancient Egypt in my own time, and the pile of books beside my bed are often about ancient Egypt.)

When I finally got to Egypt at the age of twenty, I found I could understand some of the writing on the obelisks, stelae, and coffins. I was my tour guides' delight! I really felt at home in Egypt—as if I belonged: a very odd feeling indeed. Especially interesting were the flowers decorating the architecture, and the use of floral symbology. The Amarna period was the most fascinating—this was only a short period in Egypt's long history, but I was inspired by its decorative use of naturalistic plants, flowers, and other symbolic elements. The way the ancient artists used flowers to represent the culture and times is truly clear and incredibly beautiful to me. This is what I took away most from my trip, and what I continued learning about and focusing on.

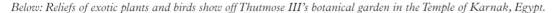

Below: Reliefs of exotic plants and birds show off Thutmose III's botanical garden in the Temple of Karnak, Egypt.

Above: An example of the floral collars from Tutankhamun's Funeral Exhibition. Dating back to 1336–1327 BC, the collar was made from papyrus, olive and persea leaves, nightshade berries, and possibly celery, as well as faience (ceramics) and dyed red linen.

With all this in mind, it's no surprise that today I preserve flowers. I cannot express how inspiring it was to see flowers that had been preserved for thousands of years. Those captured, everlasting blooms symbolized a great deal to me. They emphasized how my interests turned into my art, and I realized that this interest had always been there, lying dormant. It is not where it began or ended, but the ancient Egyptians' obsession to preserve everything never left my mind, nor, I imagine, ever will.

Early on in our relationship, Mark and I took a trip to New York together. To my delight there were two extremely spectacular exhibitions running, both about my favorite period in ancient Egypt—the Amarna period. Tutankhamun's Funeral Exhibition at the Met particularly inspired me. The ancient jars had been opened and the contents displayed—dried flowers, beautiful collars made from woven florals—and they had lasted thousands of years! I was hooked. Seeing them cemented my interest in

dried flowers: I wanted to create my own forever flowers. These would be different, of course, since they are modern, but always inspired by those ancient, preserved flowers that I was lucky enough to see with my own eyes.

Once all my formal studies were completed, I had to choose which path to take—I needed to take a leap of faith in myself. So instead of going and working for someone else's company, I started tentatively working for myself. At first, this took the form of small jobs for friends and local businesses kind enough to let me create floral work for their retail stores, spaces, weddings, and events. Later, my husband joined me in my creative—and, at the time, very risky and niche—company: we became Mark Antonia Ltd., quite simply us.

To my delight, our business name is a small nod to ancient Egypt and our family. Mark Antony (Cleopatra's calamitous lover) had a daughter named Antonia, and my father was named Antony. What seems simple in name is also rather symbolic for us. Since my father died when I was only eighteen, having him as a small part of our business name means a great deal to me. I am preserving what I have lost, through floral design. Making beauty out of sadness has been a huge part in dealing with that loss and grief, preserving his memory as I preserve my flowers: to last forever.

Initially, the work I was making was all fairly classic fresh floral pieces—bouquets, posies, garlands, etc.—predominantly for weddings, corporate events, and editorial pieces. I was able to create these in my own style, which was quite loose and whimsical at that time. However, I quite quickly became dismayed at the level of wastage involved with fresh floristry, and started exploring methods to salvage and dry the "waste" that was left over from these jobs. I would hang literally everything that was left over in our house, wherever I could. With ropes hung from every space, walking into our house looked like I was creating an upside-down garden of drying material.

The resulting dried florals started to work naturally and well. They gave me the

Left: Mark Antonia Ltd—a husband and wife team may not work for everyone, but it does for us.

Above: Who wouldn't want to work in an office that looks as good as this?

confidence to start buying flowers for the sole purpose of drying. Quite quickly I found I had a lot of material at my creative disposal, and I soon found myself searching for more things to dry. A trip down to Mark's family home, set in a huge garden on a small farm, found me more outside than in, searching for interesting things like moss, twigs, trees, and sometimes Mark's mother's prized roses, which I would take home and dry.

With all this dried material around me, I started snipping off interesting leaves, or particularly beautiful buds, which I combined together to create sculpture-like pieces. So began my love for ikebana: referencing the stylized and minimal approach of the Japanese art of flower arranging. I was truly inspired again and became soaked in that historic knowledge, using it to inform what I was creating.

Over time, my clients started choosing a mixture of dry and fresh combined. This worked magically for a while, but soon the dried work outweighed the fresh work, and I wasn't really enjoying the time-limited stress of it any more, so I was forced to choose. I decided to focus purely on dried flowers, and I think I chose well. By exploring the endless possibilities, I could create work that was new, a real leap from the traditional flowers I had been doing. Best of all, I discovered that I was not constrained so tightly as I had been with fresh flowers.

Dried flowers offer so many more possibilities for creation. I had found my niche, and now I continue to grow, make, and explore—continually experimenting and pushing myself creatively.

I am fortunate to have made a job that I love and will always love. My dried-floral history will continue to grow as I do. I will forever be exploring new techniques, styles, and design. I will never be bound by the rules, even if I have my own. I plan to always offer more, and that will keep my inquiring mind interested and engaged.

Above: I've chosen to work with dried flowers rather than the time limitations of freshly cut arrangements.

Right: This typifies my ikebana style. The leaves and flowers have been stuck to the bare stems. See page 37.

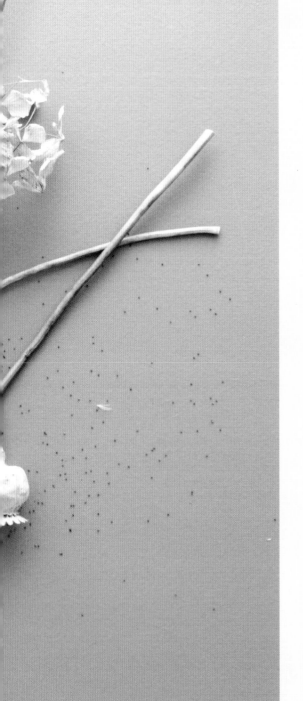

MY STUDIO

FINCH STUDIO

When I first began working with flowers, I set myself up a home studio in the second bedroom of our small flat. I had trestle tables against two of the walls, piled high with vases full of twigs and dry bunches of flowers, leaves, and other bits, all towering around a little space left clear for work. Against the other walls I had a couple of tall shelves stacked full of books, little vases, frogs, and floral accessories, as well as other unrelated but interesting inspirational things. From the ceiling we suspended ropes right across from one side of the room to the other like giant spiderwebs. On these I hung up to dry all my samples and fresh materials—alongside already dry bunches that simply had nowhere else to live.

Below: Ready for work—florals and foliage, kenzans and clippers, twine and vase

Right: Colorful, delicate and individual—and the flowers look good too!

KINGSLAND WAREHOUSE

I soon needed more room than could be provided at home. The solution proved to be an old warehouse nearby, whose lease we were able to share with another creative company that also needed more room to expand. The warehouse was by no means beautiful but was a great industrial-looking canvas for my flowers, and—once we had liberally spread putty pink paint everywhere—the huge space felt a bit warmer and softer and more like my kind of studio again.

We tried a few different shared layouts as each of us struggled for more room: my flowers often won, and eventually we had a wall built down the middle that split the warehouse into two defined spaces with a little shared showroom at the front. Now I could work in the way I wanted—a quiet private space to create, so I could concentrate on the job in front of me. At last I had lots more space to hang drying materials—wall space, ceiling space, a mezzanine—and I have used every inch; even the back of our studio front door has been covered in drying florals!

As in my home studio, I still have shelves—just many more: some filled with all the small and interesting bits and things I've found, and some dedicated to just clipped flower heads, leaves, and berries. They show a beautiful spectacle of candy colors (possibly I was subconsciously recreating my childhood candy store again!). There are even more shelves used as a stock-storing area with buckets full of my bulk-dried florals and foliage.

Below: Drying space is an essential for anyone who wants to work with flowers. It needs to be cool and well ventilated. See pages 58–59 for details on how to air-dry the flowers you pick.

Above: My work place—1. Handy tool and materials storage;
2. Keep pencils and glue sticks where you can find them easily;
3. Don't let your twine get tangled!; 4. Lazy Susan with the start of an
ikebana-style arrangement. Note the kenzan is anchored for stability
and the Japanese scissors; 5. The raw materials have been prepped and
separated, the individual leaves in glass jars. See pages 24–25.

I have lots of wall space dotted with a few large hooks for hanging my collections of bare branches and twigs off the floor and out of the way. In addition, I have space for a huge work desk just for making, with an area for all my everyday tools, plus a main space with a spinning tray (we call it a lazy Susan here) that is used for making 360-degree pieces. But still I fill out the space with piles of everything, or, rather, material that I can't throw out but don't yet know where to store—anything that may be destined for some as yet unknown purpose, alongside the expected stems and blooms.

Under my desk I keep stacks of specially dried, delicate flowers that I use only for very special jobs, all safely tidied away in huge plastic storage boxes. As well as drying racks on the walls (and door), we also use the ceiling beams above the mezzanine to suspend drying ropes. With this space full of drying and dried

flowers and foliage, it looks pretty amazing. But above all, and most importantly, the warehouse provided a larger open working space at a time when I was starting to do quite large-scale work. This has proved essential. It allows me to view projects from every angle as I assemble them, and also to move around them without damaging the delicate materials. Finally, there's space enough to move projects from the warehouse to our van without breaking them.

WHAT I'VE LEARNED FROM MY STUDIO

I like my studio to be a visual library of material. The world is my oyster in terms of what I can use in my work, and having everything around me is inspirational. It also allows me to see what I actually have, and in turn that informs my work.

Having a library of available flowers makes my job as a designer/maker much easier and provides a more fluid work process. I can easily check to make sure that my drying is working, and if not, I can try a different technique—or if that fails, grudgingly add it to the compost heap. As a visual artist, it is also so much easier to work like this. I find an observable library of flowers and foliage makes me more creative.

Having a functional studio space is crucial to my work: without it, I wouldn't be able to produce as many floral works as I do or create the large installations that quite literally can take over our entire studio. Getting these out of the studio can be quite a logistical challenge—sometimes I really do regret putting a huge pile of twigs in the wrong place.

I generally have all my wall-mounted drying racks along one straight wall that has good airflow from one end to the other, while all my dried flowers and foliage are stored directly behind or beside my working desk, so that I can easily grab something when I need it. Shelves upon shelves are filled with bunches of dry material. I try to keep like with like, but often it gets all tangled up together in a beautiful floral explosion. And as much as I try to see all my material, piles of dried florals on these shelves often hide some unused beauties that I discover only when trying my best to organize the space again to make way for new, freshly dried varieties. Or sometimes, when the shelves are too full, something buried that I have missed falls out, providing an unexpected and truly fortuitous surprise!

Beside all the dried bunches, I usually keep my shelves of apothecary jars full of the leaf clippings, buds, flower heads, and other bits that I have prepped. The flowers in these jars always fascinate customers coming into the studio, and luckily this area is probably my most organized—and also arguably the most intriguing area to take in. The jars are always stacked up on top of one another and filled with all sorts of colorful floral gems, waiting to be used.

Below: I find the best way to store smaller flowers and materials is to keep them in stackable jars. Glass jars mean you can easily find the items you require, and this way they are already prepped for use and can be easily transported to the work area.

Below: The tools of the trade! As a working florist, my store is large enough to accommodate all requirements . . . I hope!

My work table also tends to be a reflection of my greater studio state. It can be either neatly organized or completely taken over by flowers going into or left over from a particular job—or sometimes several on the go at the same time. I've noticed that it is usually most littered with leftover bits that have been prepped if I have been making an ikebana-inspired arrangement. I'll gather them all up and individually store the little cut leaves or trimmed flowers, adding them to my apothecary jar collection, rather than throwing anything out.

While my worktable is large, how quickly the space I have is gobbled up by demanding flowers waiting to be used! I make my flowers sound a bit like living creatures, and I guess they are to me. They seem as if they have their own personality—or perhaps it's mine coming through in my work.

I'm sorry to say that I'm not always organized, and it can be difficult to see all my materials. I really do have a lot—often it is absolutely brimming over the studio, seemingly wanting to explode into the street. I always need more space than the room I have, but I can't help hoarding good material when I have it. I do try, or at least aspire, to keep everything organized, but more often than not, especially after a big job, everything is everywhere and my working space becomes a minefield of dried flowers, foliage, twigs, and branches. The floor often becomes a temporary home for my acquired masses of material, which to my horror often gets walked upon! But if I see a particularly alluring fallen tree or a mass of material that I know I'll use, I'll take it all and, since the studio is already filled to the brim, squeeze it in to whatever spare space I can find.

Admittedly, I do try to keep too much floral and foliage material on hand, but still I can't help but hoard good material when I see it— it's a double-edged sword: it means I always have more variety in my studio, so more options to use all year round. Generally, I try to keep dried material from all seasons at my disposal, so I'm not limited to seasonal floral demand as much as other floral artists.

OTHER PARTS OF THE STUDIO

The tools I use most live in the pink toolbox on my desk; otherwise I'm inclined to lose them somewhere in the studio—usually under a pile of flowers. To contend with this, I have multiples of everything—tools stashed everywhere—but I often forget where they are! Tools that are needed occasionally are kept nearby but still easy to get to.

Smaller things such as glue guns, pliers, secateurs, etc. live in baskets on a shelf beside me, and larger tools such as our pole chain saw, extendable pruning snips, and ladders lean in a tool nook against the wall. There are also a few cupboards full of floral supplies—items such as ribbons, glue, tape, paper, and so on, all of which I have learned to keep in good supply. I might not be using all these tools and supplies every day, but if I do need to use a particular wire or ribbon, I don't have to worry about going out and buying them—providing I can locate them! This is particularly important since the studio is an hour out from the city center near the coast.

Within my studio I have a spray booth. It's quite unsightly to be honest, but without a sectioned-off area to paint flowers, the whole studio would be covered in paint, and it would become a rather toxic health hazard. It is also so much easier to have a dedicated painting area for flowers—I don't have to worry about what the weather is doing. In the past I often painted outside, but I quickly learned that this wasn't very practical when it was raining or a particularly strong wind sent the flowers flying down the street.

I often got paint all over myself—in my hair, on my clothes, and I ruined quite a few pairs of shoes: most of my clothing had (still has) splodges of paint somewhere. Even with a dedicated space for spraying, I can still get it all over myself, just not quite as much.

Mark and I share a designated area to photograph our work for our social media and website. I photograph all of my finished creations, which helps me keep a visual scrapbook. Customers can look at my previous work online and make choices and decisions that I can incorporate into their commissions. I also find having photos of everything I make helps me guide customers about what I can creatively achieve for them or their project.

I keep lots of vases for use in my photos, I have a vast collection of beauties that I refuse to part with. Some vases I am particularly attached to (and perhaps have too many of), but they are beautiful and useful to have in the studio.

Above: I'm a vase collector. The right vase will add immeasurably to an arrangement.

Right: Aren't they beautiful? A wall of drying flowers in my gorgeous warehouse office cannot help but attract customers.

When I'm making an arrangement, a customer will often have a specific vase that they want used. Ideally, I make the arrangement directly into that vase, but if a customer is unable to get the vase to me, I'll use a similar-sized one from my own collection. This helps inform me in the making and—most importantly—having a vase to use means I will always get the height and width right. Scale is so important in my work. In other words, I regard my vase collection as an essential tool of the job. But they also look beautiful in the studio, and I love to see them and imagine how I can use them to show off their best aspect.

FLORAL STYLES
AND MY WORK
PROCESS

I have been working with dried florals for over a decade now. In the early days I was often asked to create work that would last for as long as possible, since a fortnightly fresh arrangement was a luxury some clients could not afford. To accomplish this, I really had to think about what would suit each project—what the arrangement was trying to do and what my clients wanted me to bring out of that space. My job was to guide the customer and create an arrangement based on that agreed-on idea.

My arrangements last: this is the guiding principle behind my work. The notion of preserving anything is attractive, especially a beautiful flower or a particularly beautiful leaf, but that's only part of the plan. The work has to suit a client's ethos and branding or highlight a color in their collection.

Flowers need to be comfortable in their allotted space, and they need to complement the brand or client—to align with them personally. Dried flowers last, so a lot of the arrangements I make go across the country and internationally—my flowers are forever, after all—so they ship just fine.

My ikebana-inspired arrangements are especially popular, and I try hard to ensure that none of my arrangements duplicate my or someone else's work. In truth, I find it hard to copy my own work for client requests, so I try to decline such offers and instead give my customers a unique piece of floral art. My canvas, so to speak, is provided by the twigs, the flowers, and the paint.

In writing this book, I am also taking back that narrative and giving readers permission and guidance to make their own work, using mine as inspiration. The result should be like some of my lessons, teaching you how to make your own arrangement without having to come to one of my classes.

Enjoy creating from the comfort of your own home!

Below: Wreaths are a versatile decoration and not just for Xmas. This simple but effective wreath is made up of over a hundred tightly packed rosebuds.

Right: An ultrapop ikebana-style arrangement. It's made from twigs, billy buttons, statice flower heads, and nigella seed pods glued onto suitably selected branches.

Where do I get my inspiration? Inspiration can emerge from all sorts of things, and that comes out in my work. There is an extensive thought process behind every one of my pieces, big or small. My ikebana-inspired—I call it ike for short—work looks simple, but also complex because of the choices and combinations of natural material. However, changing the color of the material offers more creative options for your floral arrangements—and this can be achieved by using paint sprays.

I habitually splice so many different plant varieties together for my work that I'm often asked, "What's that flower?" The usual answer is that it's about five or six different varieties, glued, attached, or spliced together. I don't always get it right! I needed gold flowers once, and instead of using paint I painstakingly painted the leaves in ombre gold from makeup brand MAC (most probably). They were beautiful and natural but somehow not right.

The nature of my work is diverse, and I like to keep it interesting and fresh. I want to create new ideas, not rehash the same one repeatedly. I prefer to be challenged, by my clients and by myself. I try to explore my styles and always try new techniques or materials whenever I can.

There are many different floral styles: I tend to use my own ideas or use a new take on an existing style that I have reinterpreted. I often take styles from the past and change or alter them in ways that I find fit with my ideals. In the styles that follow, keep in mind that they are my take on the subject and my creative interpretation.

It's important to concentrate, because so much of the work is very delicate and fussy. This may sound completely contradictory, but I often find listening to a podcast or a book at the same time really helps me, and if listening to music, I like to sing along.

Above left: Ikebana is a style where less is more. Its effectiveness relies on the clever use of space and form—not volume!

Left: Wreaths do not need to be filled with flowers and foliage; keep some of the structure bare for an elegant touch.

Right: Now this is volume, but it is balanced by an understated and structural cylindrical vase. The bulk comes from ferns, pampas grass, and phylica (featherhead).

IKEBANA STYLE

Ikebana is the highly refined Japanese art of flower arranging. Here, space and elegance are every bit as important as the actual plant material. Line, form, and color are all significant, and every element is symbolic. In Japanese ikebana, seasonality is important, as is the environment in which the arrangement is going to be placed. The arrangement is not always placed in a vase but on or in a supporting structure. The plant material is bent and trimmed to harmonize with the overall intention of the maker. The emphasis is on precision, and less is often more.

In my work I have borrowed tremendously from Japanese ikebana floral art and am totally inspired by it. I'm fascinated by the techniques of the past and take note of interesting artistic movements. I know I learn more from the past than the present. Try for yourself: study the work of the old masters and gain inspiration. It has worked for me.

This style is simple and peaceful, and every single flower or leaf is considered as part of an entire whole. Ikebana arrangements are often made to sit quietly and complement the space in which they're displayed. They do not fight or take over a space. Artfulness is important. Think about what you are doing. Time is unimportant. You cannot rush an ikebana design. Even though I make ikebana arrangements to sell (and obviously have time constraints), I know that it is important not to hurry and always to give more attention to this style of arrangement than over a mass of flowers.

I also know from experience how long these ikebana-style arrangements take to make. Be patient. It has taken me over a decade of working experience to pick up skills and hone them. With experience comes the confidence to try out new techniques and the appreciation of what needs to be improved further.

I am also inspired by the *wabi-sabi* notion of treasuring something even if it's not perfect, for there is beauty in imperfection, especially with flowers. I might not always have

Below: This ikebana-style arrangement combines white helichrysums and yellow yarrow. They have been glued onto carefully chosen stems. The display is balanced by a simple complementary-colored Japanese shino-glazed vase and spiky foliage.

Above: The Ryōanji garden in Kyoto, Japan, is the one of the most famous examples of a rock garden and is considered by many to symbolize the aesthetic concept of wabi-sabi—*simplicity, understated elegance, and authenticity.*

the perfect dried flower, but sometimes it is the imperfection that's most interesting or beautiful. Within my studio, I collect and keep dried material that might not be appropriate for the current job, but I hang onto it, knowing I'll use it down the track in something else: maybe months, maybe my next project. I hardly ever throw anything out; even if it sits for a bit, that gives me time to think how best to use it.

I think ikebana arrangements are best when they are very simple. While a lot of work goes into them, they must still follow a formula that provides some structure: ikebana emphasizes shape, line, and form. However, I like to incorporate unexpected materials: in the past I have used pearls, rose quartz, and even cashmere, to name just a few different elements.

Start off with the right-sized kenzan (flower frog; *see page 33*). Since there are many sizes, but I always choose the one that best suits the finished size of an arrangement. Ikebana produces

small pieces of floral art that are intended to be kept for a very long time. They are treasured—I have kept some of mine from eons ago! Nothing has changed in the arrangements; they just last and last.

These arrangements need only simple tools: a good glue gun, knife, and small, sharp scissors—my own are Japanese bonsai steel scissors. These are so sharp they can give you a particularly good cut. I have been through many glue guns and have even gotten used to getting burned. Occasionally I use green floristry wire to bind or splice material together, creating a hybrid of sorts.

I always start with the bones—the twigs, branches, and stems—that make the framework of the arrangement. Getting the form of the composition right is important before placing any flowers and leaves. I like to use at least three different varieties of twigs to create the form I'm after. You should experiment: certain branches just look better than others.

The shape of these arrangements is vital. Don't worry if you make mistakes—judging the shape by eye comes with practice and confidence.

Once the base is ready, then comes the fun part: choosing the dried flowers and leaves. While for my work this is often my customer's choice, you have the freedom to make your own decisions and can use whatever you like. It can be helpful to select with a theme in mind.

My ikebana techniques

I modify and add to nature. I deconstruct flowers and leaves and use a glue gun to stick them onto branches and twigs to create or add to an arrangement. I go further than this. To add color that dried flowers cannot provide, I use paint. I like to use something completely natural in an unexpected way, often by picking flowers apart to make a composite that does not grow in nature. The beauty with this creative process—one of my favorites—is that you can always come up with a new spin.

Keep in mind, however, the space you intend these creations to inhabit. In business, reward comes from a happy client whose piece fills the intended location. I have learned only too well that you must make sure you think about the space where you intend to place your ikebana.

Before I touch my glue gun and glue any flowers or foliage to an arrangement, I make sure every bit of material is prepared. Prep—or, to emphasize, PREP!!!—is the most laborious side of creation, but without proper prep an arrangement can go astray. Start with the twigs/branches first; pull off any leaves or buds that you do not want in the work. Next, sort out the scale of the twigs and place them in a kenzan—this shows the bones, which helps inform how much material you will need for your arrangement. Don't fight with the stems. Use the material that best suits their inclinations. This all comes with practice!

Once the stem base is ready, prep the flowers and leaves. Cut everything in advance so that you can glue straight away, rather than having to cut as you go. Lay the material in groups: this will also help you see whether the choice of flowers and foliage works well together and is visually pleasing.

Then it's all about the gluing. Always glue leaves first to create a base, then add the flowers. Do so unevenly to give the impression that they have grown like this. Ikebana arrangements always look best when you can trick the eye—an uneven but considered design.

Above: Always consider the background to the arrangement—particularly color and texture. Here, the subtle tones of the foliage really sing out from the surrounds. The kenzan supports the display well, but some would find it unsightly. To hide it, choose a suitable vase or, perhaps, some decorative foliage.

Left: I glued two different types of rosebuds onto wiry stems to create this look.

I always keep my worktable clear for each piece I'm making. Everything is laid out, waiting to turn into something beautiful. Having a bit of space around is a practical requirement: trust me, a twig in the eye is not very pleasant!

One way I achieve the colors that I can't get from nature is by painting my florals. Since flowers are preserved and, therefore, dry, they can take all types of paint. I have experimented with many different kinds. The rainbow colors of my arrangements cover the full spectrum. I have tried floral sprays, makeup, nail polish, graffiti paint, house paint, and oh so many more types.

Experience has shown me that the best paint to use is the range that offers the most color options and textures. I now mostly use graffiti paints, since the palette selection is superb. The amazing thing about these paints is that they can be controlled—the nozzles that come with the spray can make a fine mist or a heavy color blocking. Adding painted colors to the work will lead you down a path of so many more creative opportunities. Not only this, but painting has added benefits—the painted floral lasts longer! By painting flowers, more lifespan is added, more "Foreverness."

One other aspect of the display needs to be stressed. The way you display your work is extremely important and can change the whole nature of the work. For example, a huge vase or a brighly colored one can really change an arrangement. Experiment with a range of vases and see what works best.

Left: Wall pieces like this can be as big or small as you want—just make sure that the colors of the arrangement don't disappear into the background.

Above right: For this wide-splaying type of arrangement, make certain that the vase is well weighted.

Right: Interestingly, twisted stems add real dynamism to an arrangement.

COTTAGE

Cottage garden flowers are the familiar old-fashioned plants grown for centuries outside simple dwellings. Flowers such as marigolds, stocks, roses, delphiniums, lavender, and pinks would be mixed in with herbs and vegetables in a colorful, chaotic riot of color and bloom. Many of the plants had a medicinal use that the cottager would resort to when needed: some of this knowledge has been lost or set aside in modern culture—often to our loss. The cottage style of arranging is best done with these old favorites, however, and usually there is no place for modern, overbred cultivars (although I must admit I enjoy using unusual flowers in my collage arrangments).

Inspiration for these cottage-style arrangements comes from past and present. I find dried florals from the 1970s and earlier helpful. I look at Victorian notions of flowers and their meanings, but I am also inspired by the present. Look at the abundance of nature surrounding us. Watch the beautiful color changes over the seasons and capture them through drying.

I also like to add my own interpretation to the floral art and provide a different spin to my cottage arrangements. For example, add a personal stamp with a dried lavender-scented bouquet, use ikebana-inspired elements, or paint some materials. I love creating from foraged material. Even weeds are beautiful—don't be afraid to use controversial material!

Right: Cottage style takes old favorites and allows simple displays such as this, centered on a hydrangea head and yellow yarrow.

Below: Larkspur, lavender, statice, and poppy heads—all combined into an informal bouquet.

Although cottage-inspired, don't limit yourself with a tight boundary of rules. This style of work often includes rural elements, but play with the endless artistic opportunities. A cottage arrangement can be quite seasonal, especially with foraged material. The cottage work I do in summer often has a beachy, sunshine look, because we live right by the sea and its beauty is exceedingly difficult to ignore! Fall cottage work tends toward rusty and warmer tones, while winter and spring leans toward the paler, pastel ranges. Sometimes a cottage arrangement needs to be bolder and darker, especially in the winter months. This can be achieved by using darker-hued flowers and paints—sometimes a black hydrangea or a rust-colored billy buttons (craspedia). Color is a huge aspect of all floral arrangements, but especially cottage arrangements.

Preparing to make a cottage arrangement is usually far simpler than for, say, ikebana-style works. Still, there is some prep that is especially important, so spend some time ensuring everything is ready to be used.

- Always make sure the lower parts of the stems are bare, with no foliage or flowers left. Snip off anything unsightly and dethorn those dried rose stems—dried rose spikes are so much more vicious than fresh ones! This will also makes things much easier when you put the arrangement into a vase.

- Lay everything out in groups of material. Organized like this, it's far easier to see what you have and to use it accordingly. Again, seeing the material laid out in front of you will also help you decide the size and style of a dried bouquet before you start.

- You also need twine or some type of string to bind the bouquet: this, too, is best cut before starting to make the arrangement, because your hands will be full, and having it ready is a relief when your wrist can start to feel sore from holding all your work.

I have noticed that a lot of my cottage-inspired work is in bouquet form. If it is extremely large, I tend to use eco foam or a large frog to hold the shape. I prefer to make cottage flowers into a bouquet style—it's adaptable, and traditionally they make good gifts.

Much of the work in cottage-inspired design does depend greatly on the material being used. Try not to fight and struggle with floral and foliage stems. Don't extend them beyond their capacity or twist them in extremely unnatural ways. Try to let them breathe—even though the flowers are essentially dead! Let clusters of smaller flowers exist to create visual interest,

Above: An informal cottage posy like this can be every bit as effective as an arrangement in a vase. The spiky teasel—a hedgerow plant—dries in the wild at the end of the season and works well naturally colored, as here, or painted.

and give the taller material room. I don't squish bouquets too tightly. I always find the stronger my grip, the denser and smaller the resulting arrangement. They can also be flatter than I would like—too 2-D. It's better to aim for 3-D or a 360-degree display.

Make sure that stems are left bare apart from the parts intended to rise above the vase. This avoids a dense amount of material in the wrong place at the wrong time. Other than making it a bit unsightly in a clear glass, it's also harder to accommodate it all into a vase. When making dried forever florals, always think about the ease with which the bouquet can be handled and best put into a vase. On the plus side, this work is often quicker to make than some of the other arrangements, since it rarely calls for any gluing.

I usually make a base with foliage and other more filler-type materials. Once I have my base, I can begin threading in the flowers or interesting dried finds. I can keep it traditional or change it up. With cottage arrangements, I never mind the flowers doing what they will above their stems. Flowers naturally want to go their own way, and that is that! Use this tendancy as a feature of cottage arrangements, since that flower obviously wants more days in the sun—even if it is only artificial lighting!

Once the design is in place, and before I tie it off, I always turn the arrangement to check every angle. Aim for points of interest all the way round the arrangement, not just at the front—particularly if it's intended for a table and will be viewed from all sides. A cottage arrangement can really soften a space, but think carefully before you finalize it.

Having expressed my enjoyment of the traditional, I admit that, perversely, I love to create cottage arrangements that do not necessarily use traditional cottage flowers and foliage. Indeed, some of the flowers I use are New Zealand natives—originating a long way from the traditional English cottage. The important thing to remember is that there are no hard and fast

Below: This composition of hydrangeas and lavender has been made using a technique known as spiraling. See pages 64–65.

rules. I often add an "ike" element to my arrangements as well. A great deal of the enjoyment can come from reinventing the traditional cottage bouquet for modern times. Use whatever material you want—I do, and I hate being hemmed in by restraints, especially my own!

When untraditional elements are added, the arrangement automatically becomes more modern and often more relevant design-wise. Personally, I don't want to be a florist who simply re-creates what's been done before; I want to be an artist who uses flowers as my material. This becomes evident in my cottage/ike mixes. Two styles together—and it works. Try it for yourself.

Left: The subdued and complementary colors of vase and foliage give an air of calm and femininity to this cottage bouquet.

Below: Statice, a.k.a. sea lavender, in a simple bold color makes an unmissable statement for attention!

ULTRAPOP

Ultrapop is a style of flower arrangement that emphasizes bold color, both in intensity and arrangement. Natural dried flowers and foliage rarely hold their original strong color, but this can be added artificially with the use of paint. The aim is a dynamic, eye-catching design—definitely not for the faint-hearted or shyly retiring.

This style of arrangement falls into a category all of its own, not because of the technique or the look of the finished arrangement, but for the color. Color is the most important word for ultrapop work—indeed, ultimately the colors I choose to paint the dried flowers are why I consider ultrapop my own style. I must have used every color under the sun in these arrangements.

My preferred way of adding color is by using graffiti paint. It lasts brilliantly and comes in more colors than a rainbow. I can really match an exact color quite easily, and from using so many, I also know which colors will best suit a particular job

or an arrangement. Being able to be so color specific means that the possibilities are endless. For clients I can create an arrangement to exactly match their color branding or collection demands. The style can use many colors or just a few and be used in contrast with naturally dried floral colors when wanted. So much creativity can be achieved just through color alone.

Painting, however, isn't straightforward, and there are dangers you need to be aware of. I have some epic painting gear: jumpsuits, hazmat—everything. No one wants a fainting floral maker! And I do understand the impact that spray paint causes to the environment. This is why I would only ever use sprays on forever flowers. The fact that they last eases my sleep at night a little. I can't wait for the day when these paints are more environmentally friendly. I'm on the waiting list!

While the techniques I use in making flowers vary considerably, my most popular styles of ultrapop are definitely color-blocked bouquets, but I also like fully painted ikebanas, or the elements

Below: Never underestimate the power of mirror-image arrangements. Here, all the plant material has been spray-painted pale pink.

of ripped-up flowers or foliage glued on natural ike stems. The available colors and shades are endless. The choice really does depend largely on whom it's for. I have my own favorites, which I often use—soft pinks, red wines, and sage greens are my top three—but that list changes all the time, and likely next week I will have a new color inspiring me.

I have made ultrapop arrangements with so many different things: glitter, neon lights—you name it, just in case they were not noticeable enough! And as much as I enjoy these standing out, I am also thrilled when the color is so close it becomes part of a place. One that is quite a favorite (I keep it at home) is a sage color-blocked arrangement that is the exact color of my stools. It just belongs. And when I decorate my Christmas tree, I often do so with thousands of ultrapopped flowers—a Mark Antonia Christmas tree is never a traditional one!

Below: There's no missing this colorful beauty. Note that the tones all complement each other, so while it's bright, it's not clashing.

INSTALLATIONS

These are works on a much-grander scale that absolutely command attention. Creating large work is every bit as much fun as smaller-scale work. Variety is everything and leads to continued creativity. It keeps my job interesting, a Gemini must.

Commercial installations vary much in style: so many different clients and so many different needs. More often than not, they are commissioned to be a huge focal point in an interesting space. I have been lucky enough to work on some huge installations, which still hang and act like large floral artworks. They really do alter the feel and look of a space. These flowers often become part of that company's branding or at least separate their space and business from others.

Ikebana-style installations take the most time, prep, and making. Oh, but the finished result is magical to see when it all comes together! And, surprisingly, although these arrangements can be quite delicate, on a larger scale they are often much more robust. I know this from experience after watching with my mouth wide open as Mark dropped an installation not once but twice from a great height. Nothing but a few leaves were damaged. We were quite amazed and counted our blessings on that one!

Most of my installations tend to be cottage style, so they are denser and more dominant. They really do change a space—they cannot be ignored, which is totally the point. I use all types of material on these, but densely filled hydrangea installations are probably the most popular, although a mix of cottage and ikebana on a huge scale creates something unique.

Prep is especially important on jobs of this size. Get everything well sorted out before you start making a large installation. You really must be certain that you have enough material to use—there is nothing worse than running out of a certain dried flower when the piece is not yet finished. At the planning stage, of course, the amount of material required has to be an estimate, something you'll get better at with more experience. One thing that is essential: the preparation of the actual frame (or base) is absolutely needed before you start making floral beauty.

One of the harder parts of huge installations is the actual install! Quite often the arrangements are so large that we have to hire a truck, but we often turn up at the same time as the electrician, the builder, and other tradespeople. Working around other people can be problematic. If you are installing a large piece, it's advisable to ensure that there aren't children, pets, or—sometimes—partners around!

Occasionally we have to admit defeat, either because we can't access the site or the interior work is running behind schedule, and we are safer sacrificing installation time, if it means the flowers don't get damaged. A smothering of sawdust can be a bit of a challenge to remedy!

The worst of all the problems is when the plans are incorrect and reality is different. When you create an installation, it's important wherever possible to eyeball the location carefully yourself, measuring carefully and recording those measurements clearly. This is vital whatever the space you intend to fill: at home, for a wedding reception, or for a harvest festival.

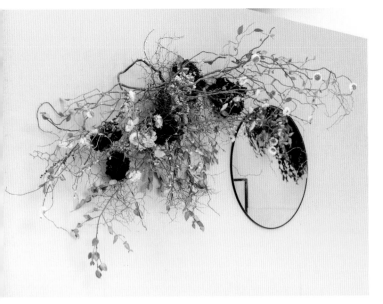

Left: This widely arcing ikebana/cottage mixed-style piece was designed with the mirror in mind. A good "prop" can make an arrangement even more effective.

Right: A good solid ladder is one of my invaluable tools and much needed for my larger installations—in this case a large ultrapop display. A statement piece like this will also need secure fastening. This is double-strapped to karabiners hanging from wire.

MARK ANTONIA LTD.

( )

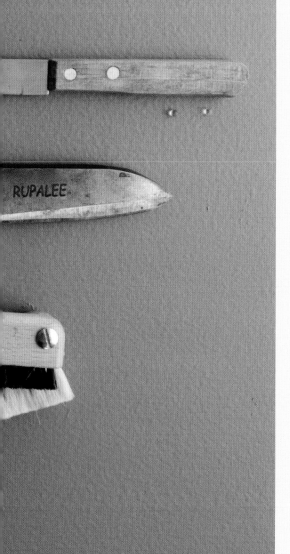

TOOLS AND TECHNIQUES

TOOLS

1. Floral foam

Floral foam is made from a combination of two chemicals (phenol and formaldehyde). Dense, lightweight, and porous, it supports flower and plant stems. It can hold up to fifty times its weight in water and is easy to cut to shape. It is useful for larger arrangements, such as installations and work that requires more density. However, it is a nonrecyclable plastic that degrades into microplastics. It is now banned (or scheduled to be) by many horticultural organizations. I try to keep my use of it to a minimum and never throw any excess out, so that I can be as sustainable as possible.

2. Floristry wire

Wire comes in a vast array of thicknesses. I prefer an exceptionally fine strand because it's bendier and easier to work compared to stronger, thicker wires. The latter are more permanent and durable but are much trickier to work without tools.

3. Garden twine

I always use twine to tie my bouquets, since it is compostable (and therefore recyclable) but also strong and sturdy. This twine comes from a local garden store—as opposed to craft twine, which tends to be weaker, breaks easily, and also costs more.

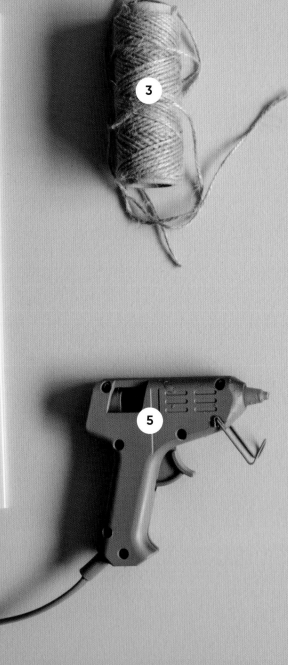

4. Glue sticks

I always use the thinner glue sticks for my work, especially for ikebana-style arrangements. They leave finer, smaller amounts of glue—the last thing you want is a big, obvious glob on your arrangement.

5. Glue gun

My glue gun is in constant use. It's the tool I use most of all in my work. I favor a generic glue gun, and because they tend to be quite unsightly, I often paint them. Without a glue gun I would not be able to neatly attach flowers and leaves to other materials. I have tried many different attachment techniques, but a hot glue gun is easily the best.

6. Japanese floral scissors

Fine Japanese bonsai scissors are essential. They are incredibly sharp and comfortable to use, and if you sharpen them regularly, they will last forever.

Tip
To keep your arrangement free of dust, simply use a hair drier set to cool and play the air stream gently over the flowers. It won't damage them and will blow the dust away.

---

7. Alternatives to floral foam

Floral foam is scheduled to be banned. It's important, therefore, to be aware of the many alternatives—although it must be said that few are as easy to use. The most obvious are pebbles, glass beads, marbles, sand, or even narrow glass tubes or vials. Other methods include the following:

- Flower frogs or kenzans (*below*). I use Japanese metal kenzan bases in much of my work and tend to favor the two styles shown here. A kenzan or spiky frog is an ikebana tool for holding up and supporting flowers. In essence, it is a small but heavy lead (sometimes weighted plastic) base with upward-protruding brass spikes. Kenzans are usually circular or square and available in various sizes.

- Wire mesh or alternative meshes made from such things as willow or reeds. The mesh allows you to use the holes to support stems.

- Wood wool, straw, or moss (very eco-friendly as long as it is ethically sourced)—these provide a dense mass into which stems can be secured.

- Floral clay. This comes in brick or tape form and may be used in the same way as floral foam, although it is denser and a little less easy to use.

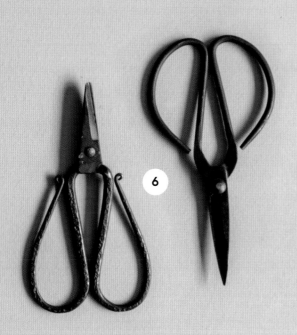

As I've mentioned, I live in New Zealand, a small island cut off from the rest of the world. As an island, we are segregated from everywhere else, and our many and native flora and fauna are different from anywhere else. Our mix of native and imported plants is vast. Even the weeds—and they do say that Auckland is one of the weediest cities of the world—provide an interesting medium. While such biodiversity gives me a true wonderland of material to use, every locality around the world has its own flora, and for those who want to practice flower arranging in the frozen North, there's always Amazon!

Drying flowers and plants is hugely enjoyable and also means that you can acquire the raw materials without recourse to shopping. Whether it's a friend's hydrangea heads or foraged material, however, it needs to be carefully dried. I learned by trial and error but with persistence and optimism. I experimented and dusted off an old book from the 1970s that had not seen daylight for decades until I pulled it from the depths of our local library. In the end, drying and trying was the best way to learn the art of drying flowers—with many experiments and failures along the way.

Drying flowers, or rather the process of it, is a bit hit and miss. Sometimes, I had unexpected success—finding a new flower that dried surprisingly well, or with little foraged experiments. There's lots to be found just in our local environs, even if those surroundings differ incredibly: interesting leaves and flowers—or weeds—of some description can usually be found in your spot of earth. Never give up on your experiments. If something doesn't work, try it another way. I implore you to explore and experiment, but with the benefit of some of my hard-learned methods.

My first advice is to start small. I did, using ordinary flowers and foliage. You can gather these easily, and this way you do not even have to spend money to start with. Go for a walk, secateurs in hand, and become inspired by what you can forage.

Below: Dried and prepped flowers ready for use on a wedding cake decoration. Such pretty pieces also make lovely mementoes.

Above: The bright yellow craspedia—billy buttons—retains its color well when dried and is a florist's favorite.

WHEN TO PICK YOUR FLOWERS

What's the best time to pick flowers for drying? Get them when you can, but it's good to get them when they are at their best. If possible, wait until midmorning, when they are sun dry after morning dew or rain has evaporated. It's best not to pick them if it's too humid or rainy, but beggars can't be choosers, and if you have to pick them when they are damp, try to gently shake off any obvious moisture. Be aware, however, that success will be hit and miss. It's also a good idea to pick them before the sun is too hot. If you can, harvest them before the end of their blooming cycle, while some of the buds aren't fully open. This way they won't drop or droop—the flowers continue to open as they dry, and if you pick them late you will lose petals. It's good for arrangements to have some buds as well.

DRYING FLOWERS

The three methods that I use for drying my flowers are detailed on the pages that follow. However, a couple of other methods also need a brief mention.

Many people use a microwave to dry flowers, but I find that the flowers can change in color or become more fragile. Often, heating and using silica on flowers can also create little pockmarks, making them look less natural. So, for these reasons I prefer not to use a microwave myself.

Early in our relationship, Mark made me a beautiful flower press. While I don't use a flower press in my day-to-day work, I often use pressed flowers to make personalised cards or presents for my friends and family.

STORING DRIED FLOWERS

You must take care of them once they are dried. While some—hydrangeas, for example—are quite robust, others—such as dried grasses—can be very brittle. You will certainly need to store them carefully, and that's probably best done in boxes or sturdy plastic containers. The key factors are that they should be cool and dry. Wrap them in newspaper or tissue paper. Don't pack them too tightly or crush them by putting heavy items on top. If the boxes are solid, label them so you know what's in each, and you won't have to keep opening them all and, therefore, shaking them up each time you search through them to find what you need.

SEALING

I do not seal my dried flowers. I prefer them to be natural. If something is particularly delicate or easily damaged, I (not very often) might use strong hair spray to seal or help hold a dried flower together a bit better. But it does not always work on every fragile flower; some are just too fragile and best used picked apart for an ikebana-style arrangement. And there is the chance of discoloring a beautiful, colored hue of a flower.

PAINTING

I use spray paints as my preferred paint. I use these, as you know, for their vast array of colors and vibrancy. These sprays also go a lot further than traditional floral sprays, which often are also more expensive and harder to find. Every flower or foliage type takes more or less of an amount of spray paint. It really does depend on what material you are coloring.

I always paint finely first; it is a bit like painting a wall—you do not want to create a thick layer. It is the same with painting flowers. So, I spray in layers and more layers. I always let the spray paint dry before I paint my next layer. Spray paint often comes with different nozzles for a fine mist or a more concentrated spray of paint. The more concentrated spray nozzles are best for getting into the harder or difficult areas to paint. Trial and error come also with painting. Sometimes you might think that you are finished painting as soon as you get these flowers out of your painting space. The light might show some areas you might have missed. Never mind; you can always spray more if need be. Often, I find that some of my work requires less paint; I sometimes let some of the natural colors of the flowers come through.

Below: Glass, airtight jars are excellent for storage and also make an unusual and eye-catching display—beautiful in their own right.

Above: Remember, you don't need to stick to nature's colors—it's your arrangement; do what you want!

The time it takes for your flowers to dry does depend on where you place them. Often, I will place a fan in front of my painted flowers. Never put a heater in front of your paint-drying flowers. It often can create an uneven texture, since this dries them too quickly.

Also, a darker bloom will take more paint coverage if it is a darker hue naturally. A lighter color will not need as much darker paint.

I do not use paints that are enamel based, since they have a smell that is rather acrid; the sprays I tend to use are acrylic based and really do not smell after long.

GLUING

My gluing technique is delicate. I only ever use a hot glue gun, since its glue is more flexible for the glued flowers. When I glue, I use as little as possible. Less is more. It is a practice of restraint. A little dab of glue is all you need. You must be quick and confident to quickly glue the flower or leaf to your arrangement. The hot glue cools quickly, and the hotter it is when you glue your material, the stronger it will stick and the better it will last and later, lasting forever.

With gluing with a hot glue gun, often more than not there are what I call spider wisps of glue. I always remove these as I make my arrangements. I always check after I have made my arrangements, to make sure I have not missed any.

Below: A glue gun is an absolutely essential tool—and I have the scars to prove it. Seriously, be very careful using them.

AIR DRYING

The easiest, and my favorite method of drying. All you need is an area with fresh air and space. A hanging twine rope is a wonderful foundation for your drying. I hang ropes everywhere I can. In the early days, any space I could find in our small house was hung with drying flowers.

Prep your flowers by removing the leaves (unless you want them), because this makes the flowers dry quicker (*pictures 1a, 1b, and 1c*). You can also see your progress better as they dry.

Try to tie your rope or twine as tightly as you can, but without breaking the stems (*picture 2*). You'll find that as the flowers and foliage dry, the stems will shrink, and you don't want your material slipping out and getting ruined.

When hanging the flowers, make sure that they have plenty of room to breathe. Because they are fresh and still contain water, they can quickly become moldy. I always stagger my flowers, keeping the stems at different lengths, so that the blooms have more breathing space and will not dry squashed flat (*picture 3*).

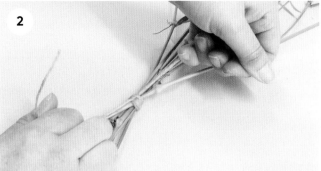

I use wall space to dry my flowers and foliage, using steel mesh against bare concrete walls that are more foundations than finished. This creates airflow on both sides (*picture 4*).

Once your material is tied, try to fluff it up so it gets as much air as possible (*picture 5*).

Now all you need to do is be patient—different material will take different times to dry (*picture 6*). The fleshier the flower, the longer it will take. Roses and berries can take quite a lot longer. Thinner, more-papery flowers, such as statice and gypsophila, will dry quicker.

SILICA DRYING

This method is for flowers that are particularly hard to dry and do not respond well to air drying. Silica gives wonderful results, and the silica I use is reusable. I can dry flowers when the beads are orange, and when the silica has taken too much water, the orange beads turn green. Then the silica is regenerated by putting it in the oven, or the microwave as a last resort. You must keep the silica drying material in airtight containers, since the silica is not interested in air, unlike air-dried flowers.

Many flowers do well in silica, even when they're fleshy. However, with trial and error, I have still found, alas, some flowers just want to remain fresh. The fleshier the flower, the harder or more impossible to dry. Think desert flowers, any flower that retrains as much moisture as possible.
I have found flowers such as dahlias and chrysanthemums are nearly impossible to dry satisfactorily.

When preparing flowers to dry in silica, always cut off the stems and keep only the blooms (*picture 1*). I have found that the fleshy stems do not dry well and, anyway, often make the flowers take longer to dry. So cut your flowers as close to the bud as possible.

Create a fine bed of silica for your flowers (*picture 2*). I always add the more robust and less delicate flowers first (*picture 3*). Separate them and try not to let them sit too close together (*picture 4*).

Now add a good covering over your first layer of flowers (*picture 5*). Don't crush them; just pour the silica in gently, covering as much of each flower as possible. They don't need to be fully coated, since this will help you see where to place

your second layer of flowers. Place them between the gaps of the first layer so that they all have as much space as possible.

Your second layer is more for the dainty and fragile flowers. Much the same as the first step, lay your flowers flat and with as much room as possible (*picture 6*). You can stack over your first layered flowers, but only if you are running out of space. (I often do!)

Now delicately cover over your second layer, even more carefully than your first layer (*picture 7*).

Your silica-covered flowers are now ready to leave alone for a week or so. Regularly check to see how they are drying, but be careful not to rip any petals, since they do become like fragile paper. Anemones and poppies are especially delicate, so handle them with particular care.

Flowers that dry the quickest in silica will be the ones that are more papery in nature. Roses and larkspur, for instance, will take a few days to dry in silica, whereas a fleshy or quite a dense flower like an orchid will take a couple of weeks to get a properly dried result. Don't worry; you cannot leave your drying flowers in for too long—the silica will simply preserve your flowers further and protect them. I often leave the flowers I do not need for a job preserved in my silica for months and months.

The finished result still always creates excitement and wonder for me. The way these flowers keep their color and shape almost makes them look like silk flowers, just more delicate (*picture 8*).

61

WATER DRYING

This method is a good one and is a complete paradox to "drying." I use this method to dry my hydrangeas that are still quite fresh when summer is not in full swing.

Hydrangea stems are like straws, in that they suck up as much water as they can. This is not helpful for drying, so they must be dried gradually with water to keep their shape; otherwise you'll end up with a shriveled hydrangea, not a perfect beautiful, dried flower head. I prefer to use nonshriveled hydrangeas, and I am sure you do too!

Hydrangeas are the only flower I dry with the water technique, because these are the only flowers I use a lot that require this. Think of it this way: any flower on which the stem looks or seems like a straw will work well with this slow water technique.

Start by cutting all the leaves off your hydrangea stems (*pictures 1a, 1b*). Cut the stems on a slant; this lets the hydrangea take in more water. The leaves just get rotten in the water and can create a nasty smell. Make sure they are all gone.

Fill a bucket, a vase, or anything that will take a large amount of water. I tend to fill mine half full. I use flower food, especially on younger hydrangea blooms to help them keep their shape; the flower food helps the flowers last longer and keep that round shape during drying. I add one sachet into the water (*picture 2*).

3

Now place your trimmed hydrangeas in the bucket (*picture 3*). I change the water every three or four days to keep the water fresh, and this lets me check on their drying progress. Every time I change the water for my water-drying hydrangeas, I do add a sachet of flower food to the fresh water.

Leave your hydrangeas to sit and soak (*picture 4*)—they usually take a couple of weeks to dry, depending on the climate. Newer hydrangea heads often do not dry as well as a hydrangea that has had more time in the sun. But I find this is one of my favorite drying techniques (*picture 5*).

5

4

SPIRALING

Prep all the stems before you begin by removing any excess leaves or thorns. While learning this technique, it can be useful to trim all the stems to much the same length to make it easier. Lay out all your material in front of you (*picture 1*).

Before you start to create your bouquet, you need to think about where you are going hold your stems as you create it, because this is where you will tie it up once finished. The higher up the stems, the tighter and smaller the finished arrangement will be. If you hold it lower down, the stems you will get a bigger arrangement.

You will hold your bouquet in the same hand throughout; one thing I have noticed when teaching spiraling classes is that a lot of people hold on to their bouquet too tightly, gripping it too much. I keep my hands loose and try to hold my bouquet with just my thumb and finger, rather than my whole hand. You can, of course, use more fingers if you find it easier. I know a lot of beginners worry that if they don't hold on to it for dear life they will lose the structure of the bouquet, but actually, the more you practice spiraling, the more you will be understand the amount to pressure you need to apply.

Begin by making a cross with your first two stems at roughly a 45-degree angle (*picture 2*).

Add and overlap a third stem at the same diagonal angle (*picture 3*). Turn the bouquet slightly, then add the next stem at the same angle. (NB: You turn the bouquet with the hand that is not holding the flowers.) Turn slightly again and repeat (*picture 4*). This layers the stems one on top of the other. The lower stems will splay out from beneath your hand. Keep turning and adding stems until the bouquet is complete (*picture 5*).

Heavier flowers may drop down in the bunch as you work due to their weight. If this is the case, gently pull them up to the height that you want with your spare hand, and then slightly tighten your grip on the bouquet so that they stay in place.

Once you have completed your bouquet, you need to tie it up (it is always handy to have a length of twine already cut and to hand). While still holding the bouquet, use your spare hand to pass the twine round the stems (as close to the hand holding the bouquet as possible). Pull the twin tight and then tie it in a bow (*picture 6*).

Last, trim all of the stems so that they are the same length (*picture 7*). The final test of a perfectly spiraled bouquet (once you have trimmed its stems) is to see if it will stand up on its own. If you have spiraled well, it will (*picture 8*).

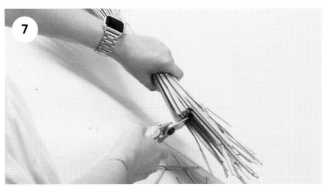

DRIED
FLOWER
DIRECTORY

SPRING

After long cold winter days of being kept indoors, spring bursts out in color and perfume. Blossoms start opening, and their scent is my favorite part of the beginning of springtime.

Everywhere the wild jasmine, freesias, daffodils, and many more flowers pop up out of the ground. They seem to have a mind of their own, and spring is up, suddenly, everywhere.

As I walk to work, I always pick a few flowers—sometimes more than I should! Here, they are so bountiful, I don't think anyone minds. Living in a rural town, almost the country, there is much to snip and cherish, filling the house with the beautiful soft scent of spring—elsewhere, I know there are restrictions that one must be careful to obey.

Certainly, no one minds me snipping and keeping weeds and many wildflowers. I find beauty in all of them, even weeds. Queen Anne's lace grows on the side of the road. I take as much as my arms can carry, and dry them. Simple hairspray makes these keep their shape. I once was asked to make arrangements for all the Jo Malone stores in New Zealand to highlight a collection of fragrances simply called "Wildflowers & Weeds." This was a project I greatly enjoyed, letting those beautiful weeds and wildflowers have a time for themselves—for the beauty that not only I saw, but the perfume house itself.

Spring brings lots of rain. Though not as heavy as a winter downpour, somehow it smells sweeter to me. It must be all those blossoms adding to the scent of the softer rain.

I refuse to wear a jacket in spring rain, since I love that fresh feeling of life on my skin. It's not cold, just refreshing, and it's not going to give me a cold. I just must make sure that I'm not wearing a white t-shirt!

I love spring; I call it the season before the silly season of Christmas (remember, I'm in the Southern Hemisphere), when I tend to be the busiest, creating my floral art for all my clients and their heartfelt Christmas presents. I gather as much material as I possibly can in spring to help with the busy months ahead.

My studio is usually crammed to the brim with drying flowers now, and people visiting the studio often comment on their scent. I feel that spring brings happiness to people, the joy of summer to come.

FLOWER AND FOLIAGE CHARTS

Flower	Drying Method
(*Consolida ajacis* and various other species) **Larkspur**	hung/air dried
(*Craspedia globosa*) **Billy buttons**	hung/air dried
(*Daucus carota*) **Queen Anne's lace / Wild carrot**	hung/air dried
(*Delphinium elatum*) **Delphinium**	silica dried
(*Dianthus*, different varieties) **Carnation / Pinks**	silica dried
(*Gypsophila paniculata*) **Baby's breath**	hung/air dried
(*Leucospermum*, various species) **Pincushions**	hung/air dried
(*Orchidaceae*, numerous species) **Orchid**	silica dried
(*Ornithogalum thyrsoides*) **Chincherinchee**	silica dried
(*Papaver*, various species) **Poppy heads**	hung/air dried
(*Pieris japonica*) **Pieris**	hung/air dried
(*Prunus serrulata*) **Japanese cherry**	air dried
(*Solidago speciosa*) **Goldenrod**	hung/air dried
(*Stirlingia latifolia*) **Blueboy**	hung/air dried
Wild flowers, various foraged species	hung/ air dried

Foliage	Drying Method
(*Acacia*, numerous species) **Wattle**	hung/air dried
(*Asparagus*, various species) **Asparagus fern / Ming fern**	hung/air dried
(*Cyatheales*, various species) **Tree fern**	hung/air dried
(*Eucalyptus pauciflora*) **Snow gum**	hung/air dried
(*Fagus sylvatica purpurea*) **Copper beech / Purple beech**	hung/air dried
(*Genisteae*, various species) **Broom / Gorse**	hung/air dried
(*Leptospermum scoparium*) **Manuka /Tea tree**	hung/air dried
(*Leucadendron argenteum*) **Cape silver tree**	hung/air dried
(*Lophomyrtus*) **New Zealand myrtle / Little star**	hung/air dried
(*Monstera deliciosa*) **Swiss cheese plant**	silica dried
(*Rhododendron*, various species) **Rhododendron / Snow rose**	silica dried
(*Salix discolor*) **Pussy willow**	hung/air dried

SUMMER

Scorched by the sun, summer is a time for an abundance of flowers and foliage. I always love the natural simplicity of the colors summer brings. With summer also comes the scent of the season, dry and fresh at the same time. I often forage in summer, excited by all its beautiful flowers just wanting to be snipped. Summer also dries the flowers for me, so I collect the fluffy pampas grass stems, browned russets, naturally dried hydrangeas, and poppy heads once the dried seeds have scattered for the next season of growth.

Summer for me is spent under the sun, enjoying summer walks, always with my secateurs, ready to forage anything of interest I see. I'm always hunting for new material to work with—looking for ideas and inspiration.

Cool wine and balmy evenings, when the sun never ceases to disappear, large hats, long cotton dresses, and coconut sunblock mix with the scent of fresh washing on the line and newly cut grass. It's a magical season to be still and relax; to take naps in the sun alternated with constant dips into the sea; for tanned skin even with ample sunblock.

It is easier to dream in this season of endless promises. Time off from a busy schedule is opportunity to reflect on the year to come. Our dreams and plans are even more possible under the sun's beautiful light.

Blankets are tossed away, replaced by lighter sheets and taller umbrellas on the balcony.

It's a time when people come together to relish each other's company; beers on the patio with summer fruits and ice cream.

Summer naturally brings us all outside: no more rain, no more cold—new friends are made or old ones made anew.

Fresh herbs on the balcony are even more scented when stirred by a gentle summer breeze; more mint—lots more mint—you can never have enough mint.

In summer I focus more on myself. Summer allows time off to gather one's self and provides time to be thoughtful and full of potential.

Barbecues dusted off, eating outdoors, evenings are longer, and time seems endless—blissful summer!

FLOWER AND FOLIAGE CHARTS

Flower	Drying Method
(*Ageratum houstonianum*) Floss flower / Blueweed / Pussy foot	hung/air dried
(*Astilbe grandis*) False goat's beard	hung/air dried
(*Bidens ferulifolia*) Fern-leaved beggar-ticks	hung/air dried
(*Celosia argentea*) Plumed cockscomb	hung/air dried
(*Combretum hereroense*) Russet bushwillow	hung/air dried
(*Consolida ajacis*) Larkspur	silica dried
(*Cortaderia selloana*) Pampas grass	hung/air dried
(*Craspedia globosa*) Billy buttons	hung/air dried
(*Delphinium elatum*) Delphinium	silica dried
(*Dierama pulcherrimum*) Angel's fishing rods	silica dried
(*Echinops bannaticus*) Globe thistle	hung/air dried
(*Eryngium bourgatii*) Mediterranean sea holly	hung/air dried
(*Eustoma grandiflorum*) Prairie gentian / Lisianthus	silica dried
(*Gomphrena globosa*) Globe amaranth	hung/air dried
(*Helichrysum bracteatum*) Everlasting flower	hung/air dried
(*Hydrangea macrophylla*) Hydrangea	water dried
(*Jasminum sambac*) Arabian jasmine	silica dried
(*Lagurus ovatus*) Bunny's tail grass/Hare's tail	hung/air dried
(*Lavandula angustifolia*) English lavender	hung/air dried

Flower (continued)	Drying Method
(*Lavandula latifolia*) Spike lavender	hung/air dried
(*Limonium sinuatum*) Sea lavender / Statice	hung/air dried
(*Nigella orientalis*) Yellow fennel flower	silica dried
(*Papaver somniferum*) Opium poppy seed head	hung/air dried
(*Rosa rubiginosa*) Sweet briar rose	silica dried
(*Xerochrysum bracteatum*) Everlasting flower / Strawflower	hung/air dried

Foliage	Drying Method
(*Artemisia absinthium*) Wormwood / Absinthe	hung/air dried
(*Asparagus setaceus*) Ming fern / Lace fern	hung/air dried
(*Chionochloa flavicans*) Broad-leafed snow tussock	hung/air dried
(*Combretum hereroense*) Russet bush willow	hung/air dried
(*Cortaderia selloana*) Pampas grass	hung/air dried
(*Cotinus coggygria*) Smoke bush / Smoke tree	hung/air dried
(*Dipsacus fullonum*) Wild teasel	hung/air dried
(Many and various species) Herbs	hung/air dried
(*Ruscus hypoglossum*) Spineless butcher's broom	hung/air dried
(*Triticum aestivum*) Wheat	hung/air dried

FALL

Fall is a time of gathering and taking what is left of summer, a transitional season.

Snipping the last of the summer roses, berries, and foliage, I find this time cathartic, preparing me for the darker months to come. I relish what I can find under the naturally dimmer, softer light.

Autumn has always been one of my favorite seasons: a time of collection and working, looking forward to the rest of the year. I find some of my favorite flowers and foliage in this time.

I collect buckets of eucalyptus leaves that have been bleached by the sun. It becomes dusty bleached pink from its once-fresh green—absolutely one of my favorite foliages that I forage across the grounds of my generous neighbors.

I love watching the green leaves of summer turn to umber and darker hues. Nature is so beautiful in every season, but fall is my favorite season to marvel at these color changes.

I offer to prune my local friends' gardens, since removing these flowers will only help the plants regenerate in the seasons to come. They are happy for me to take away what they see as dead—however, I see only possibilities, and my head is flooded with new ideas for my new material. When I forage in fall, I am always finding new plants to experiment with—I am always looking for a challenge.

It is a win–win situation for everyone!

The fires are starting to be lit again; that sweet smell of burning wood permeates the town. It is a scent I always find pleasing— especially when our native manuka wood is being burned, giving off a softer, sweeter smell.

In autumn I wash the winter blankets and my wardrobe in preparation for the cooler weather to come. And I have many treasured clothes that had been put away for summer to resuscitate!

As the beach time starts to lessen, we jump into the water for our last swims of the season.

I start buying more incense, especially Japanese incense, which sets the scene for an autumn to cherish with its softer sun and longer times indoors.

FLOWER AND FOLIAGE CHARTS

Flower	Drying Method
(*Achillea millefolium*) **Yarrow**	hung/air dried
(*Amaranthus palmeri*) **Palmer's pigweed**	hung/air dried
(*Anemone x hybrida*) **Japanese anemone**	silica dried
(*Celosia cristata*) **Cockscomb**	hung/air dried
(*Convallaria majalis*) **Lily of the valley**	silica dried
(*Echinacea*, various species) **Coneflower**	silica dried
(*Hydrangea*, various species and hybrids) **Hortensia / Hydrangea**	water slow dried
(*Limonium caspia*) **Caspia / Marsh rosemary**	hung/air dried
(*Lunaria annua*) **Honesty**	hung/air dried
(*Moluccella laevis*) **Bells of Ireland**	hung/air dried
(*Nigella damascena*) **Love-in-a-mist**	hung/air dried
(*Physalis peruviana*) **Cape gooseberry / Poha**	hung/air dried
(*Protea*, various species) **Protea / Sugarbush**	hung/air dried
(*Rosa floribunda*, various varieties) **Spray rose**	hung/air dried
(*Rosa*, various species and hybrids) **Rose**	hung/air dried
(*Scabiosa*, various species **Pincushion flower**	hung/air dried
(*Triticum aestivum*) **Wheat**	hung/air dried
(*Viburnum opulus*) **Viburnum Guelder rose**	hung/air dried
(*Xeranthemum annuum*) **Annual / Common everlasting flower**	silica dried

Foliage	Drying Method
(*Echinops bannaticus*) **Globe thistle**	hung/air dried
(*Eucalyptus globulus*) **Southern blue gum**	hung/air dried
(*Lathyrus sativus*) **Grass pea**	silica dried
(*Linum usitatissimum*) **Linseed / Flax**	hung/air dried
(*Nigella sativa*) **Love-in-a-mist seed heads**	hung/air dried
(*Phalaris minor*) **Little-seed canary grass**	hung/air dried
(*Phormium tenax*) **New Zealand flax**	hung/air dried
(*Pittosporum tenuifolium*) **Kohuhu**	hung/air dried
(*Salvia officinalis*) **Sage**	hung/air dried

WINTER

Winter, times of needed warmth and shorter days.

Flowers are few, so instead I focus on the beautiful cones and foliage I can find and dry.

I use these in many ways, but winter wreaths capture the season so beautifully.

I gather what I can, but with limitations of found flowers and foliage, I am forced to be more resourceful. This is good because I really do love a challenge. I refuse to rest on my laurels, however tempting.

In fact, the winter season can sometimes be one of my busiest, even though fresh flowers are few and far between. Since I work only with dried material, I am able to create more than traditional florists.

I love winter for its indoor comforts and being wrapped in blankets, with darker wine or a tipple of whisky giving warmth to even the coolest of evenings.

The cats come in from the outside they love, to cuddle with us—much like wriggling hot-water bottles. Sometimes our bed turns from two to four, all hunkering down to find the most warmth.

Candles are always lit, creating a calming light and an intoxicating scent. We burn our own winter candle constantly in this season. I developed this scent for Mark and our winter wedding. This scent is so nostalgic, so I always save our winter candle for these months—along with pillar candles for when the power cuts happen after a good storm.

There's more time for reading books, more time for the simple things such as hearty and nourishing longer meals. There is much you can do with lentils!

More fires are lit, heaters on full, and warmer baths.

Cuddles are also much more satisfying in winter, when you will thankfully take any loving warmth you can find or be given.

FLOWER AND FOLIAGE CHARTS

Flower	Drying Method
(*Anthurium andraeanum*) Flamingo flower	silica dried
(*Calluna vulgaris*) **Heather / Ling**	hung/air dried
(*Gardenia jasminoides*) Gardenia / Cape jasmine	silica dried
(*Helleborus x hybridus*) Hellebore / Lenten rose	silica dried
(*Leucadendron laureolum*) Leucadendron / Golden conebush	hung/air dried
(*Myrtus communis*) **Myrtle**	silica dried
(*Ozothamnus diosmifolius*) Rice flower / Sago bush	hung/air dried
(*Paeonia*) **Peony**	air dried
(*Ranunculus asiaticus*) Persian buttercup	silica dried

Foliage	Drying Method
(*Abies procera*, cones) **Abies / Noble fir**	air dried
(*Arecaceae*, leaves of various species) Palm	silica dried
(*Betula*, stems of varioius species) **Birch**	hung/air dried
(*Cupressus*, cones) **Cyprus tree**	hung/air dried
(*Cynara cardunculus*) Cardoon / Artichoke thistle	hung/air dried
(*Laurus nobilis*) **Bay tree**	hung/air dried
(*Olea europaea*) **Olive tree**	hung/air dried
(*Photinia x fraseri*) **Red-tip photinia**	hung/air dried
(*Phylica pubescens*) Featherhead /Downy phylica	hung/air dried
(*Pinophyta*, cones of various species) Conifer	hung/air dried
(*Pinus*, cones of various species) Pine cones	air dried
(*Pittosporum tobira*) Japanese cheesewood / Australian laurel	hung/air dried
(*Restionaceae*, various species) Restio grass	hung/air dried
(*Salix discolor*) **Pussy willow**	hung/air dried

Asparagus macowanii
Ming Fern

This fluffy beauty is often bought already dyed or bleached. Since asparagus grass is a nuisance weed in New Zealand, it has to be imported, unfortunately. But it is beautiful. I use white and pink mostly, but it does paint very nicely, and I use this in all my styles of work. It's expensive, but so versatile.

Craspedia globosa
Billy Buttons

The form of craspedia popularly known as billy buttons is unusual and always creates a point of difference in my work. The yellow is bold but paints well. I use this most in more sculptural work, where I let it have space and height rather than hiding it among the other flowers.

Eucalyptus camaldulensis
Eucalyptus Leaves

Such a versatile foliage; I use this in almost all my work. The sage-green leaves are beautiful, and when summer is particularly bright, they bleach to a beautiful putty pink. I use both colors extensively in my ikebana-style work, and mostly the sage-green leaves in posies and bouquets.

Gomphrena globosa
Globe Amaranth

I love these little puff balls. Gomphrena comes in so many different colors. I mostly use white and soft pink in my ikebana work and in wreaths. However, I very rarely use just a stem of it. Instead, I cut off the bloom and attach it to my work—I find I make better use out of this beautiful bud this way.

Gypsophila paniculata
Baby's Breath

This flower is so versatile, being soft and textural with small buds of beautiful white blooms. It's beautiful, both natural and colored. I often paint my gypsophila and use it in posies and bouquets or cut it into smaller sections for my ike work. It's usually really expensive here, so I always make sure that I use it carefully to get the most out of of it.

Hydrangea macrophylla
Hydrangea/Hortensia

Hydrangeas are just so versatile to use—either as a whole bloom or cut apart. I use these almost every week in my floral work. They look amazing whether in a bunch/bouquet of flowers or as single florets cut and glued onto my ikebana-inspired pieces. I love hydrangeas for the variety of ways you can use them. Furthermore, they last for ages. I always have hydrangeas on hand.

Jacobaea maritima
Dusty Miller

The silvery, velvety leaves of dusty miller are so unusual.
I often use them to create a sense of softness in my work.
Interestingly, this plant looks like it would not dry, but quite the
opposite—it dries well, just air hung. I use the yellow flowers
in bouquets, such a contrast color to its silvery leaves. It is a
plant that I use for all my work styles. My favorite use is in my
ikebana-style work, cut and glued onto twigs and branches for
an interesting look.

Lagurus ovatus
Bunny's Tail

These soft and fluffy cuties grow wild around our native
beaches and, happily, are abundant in summer. I forage as
much as I can of these for work throughout the year. They are
the favorite flower of many of my clients who request them
in their arrangements. I use these mostly in my ikebana-style
work and in wreaths and posies. As a bonus, they look lovely in
painted colors too.

Lavandula latifolia
Lavender

Still scented even when dried; I love adding lavender to my bouquets and posies. With lavender I can create a dried arrangement with a scent that will last for ages. It is a beautiful addition to my work, beauty and scent creating something really special. Lavender is calming too; I like to think that anyone with one of my lavender works will get plenty of calm and relaxation.

Limonium
Statice

My favorite statice flower color is the purple or white, although there are lots of other colors, including good blues and yellows. It's such a papery plant that it dries almost immediately. I regularly use statice in all aspects of my work, but especially dried bouquets and wreaths. It is a plant that once dried very rarely loses its color, unless in direct sun (but then, anything natural will fade in that!)

Linum usitatissimum
Linseed/Flax

Linseed has these lovely little seed heads at the top, held up in numerous bunches. So, I like to use these en masse and clustered throughout my bouquets and posies. Furthermore, linseed is easily colored, and I especially love using them when they're painted gold—it makes the grain seem more mythological and Greek, like a god's grain!

Loudetia simplex
Russet Grass

I use russet grass so much in my summer work because there are so many different types. With its natural burned color and bloom at the tip, it's beautiful whether in a summer bouquet or massive installation. I also use the buds of russet in my ikebana-style work, especially if it has a beautiful natural brass color.

Nigella orientalis
Nigella Seed Pods

These have such a striking and unusual shape, like little upside-down umbrellas. This is also a very versatile material that I use in all areas of my work. It's lovely whether natural or painted and is also great to use as individual elements or clustered together en masse.

Papaver somniferum
Poppy Heads

These are so interesting to look at, and they dry so well. I regularly use them, especially in my more cottage- or beachy-style arrangements. The form of the poppy head adds an interesting point of difference. I also use them in my ikebana-style arrangements, cutting the head off and gluing it onto the bare stems.

Phylica pubescens
Featherhead

Dried phylica is so soft and fluffy, so I use it to add softness to my work. I like to use it especially in larger works or in bouquets. It also colors well and can look even more interesting. After I've painted it, I cut off the heads and attach them onto an ikebana-inspired work, where they always contrast beautifully with the other foliage.

Rosa
Rose

I use mostly very dark-hued roses in my work. Roses in all sizes dry very well, although I use spray roses the most. The darker the rose, the better the natural dried color. They are so petite and beautiful. I regularly use dried roses in all my designs.

Scabiosa stellata
Scabious/Starflower

The form of this flower is so unusual: I love its round, spiky shape with those teeny, tiny, little flowers it's covered in. It is quite a fragile little flower, and the individual heads often break away, but I keep them and use them instead in my ikebana work. These flowers really are quite versatile, so I use them in all my work.

Triticum
Wheat

Dried wheat is so lovely to work with. I use it a lot in wreaths, bouquets, and ikebana-inspired work. It is very versatile and looks striking both individually and in clusters. Painted wheat is also a favorite of mine, and it always features in my summer pieces. I keep wheat in my library of dried flowers.

Viburnum tinus
Viburnum Berries

These little, hard berries come in a dark midnight blue and in lighter plum shades. I use these berries individually or sometimes use a whole stem of berries and leaves. They are quite fragile on their stem, so I tend to use them more in my ikebana-style work. I use the whole stem less often but in smaller compact posies. I also use their dried leaves for ikebana work.

Xerochrysum bracteatum
Strawflower

The more papery a flower, the easier it is to dry, and these papery beauties are so easy to dry! This is quite a rainbow flower, and I think I have seen it in nearly every color possible. However, I mostly use white, yellow, and pink strawflowers in my works. In addition, the natural color is so vibrant I hardly ever paint them.

STEP-BY-STEP
FLORAL PIECES

POSIES

COTTAGE POSY

A proper posy is traditional and soft in nature. They are the smaller sister of a classic bouquet but no less beautiful. Their size does not mean they are any less designed, just on a smaller scale. However, their material has to be more purposefully placed to make the most impact on a smaller style.

I enjoy the smaller scale of posies. By using less material, I find my design becomes more considered and refined. Posies are no less of a challenge despite their size. My classic posies are packed full of beautiful material without going over the top. Using less material is by no means a lacking arrangement; my maker's eye is still refined. The challenge is there for me to appreciate—I still strive to create balance and points of interest.

I use old-fashioned flowers and foliage in my classic posies—just a nod to the traditional past through dried florals. Here I have used softer material, which is contrasted with the clusters of scented lavender and eucalyptus. The soft ming fern and delicate gypsofila frame the other flowers.

Classic posies are particularly popular for weddings, especially as bridesmaid's flowers, since they are the perfect size for a bridesmaid to carry. And, of course, they can be kept long after the celebration. Because their keepsake is dried, it will not perish like a fresh posy. They are also perfect for a smaller home, or an apartment that has limited space, since they are easier to display.

MATERIALS
- **3–4 types of foliage and flowers** (preferably of different forms and sizes). Natural is best. I used sage eucalyptus, ming fern, hydrangea, gypsophilia, and scented lavender.
- **sharp scissors**
- **twine**

Step 1:
Start with the base of foliage first (in this case, the sage eucalyptus and the white ming fern): this provides the bones of the arrangement.

Since this posy style does not need a great deal of material, I use shape, clustering, and space to create interest. Spiraling is a florists' technique that needs skill, so I am not going to add it here, since you don't need to spiral immediately to create beautiful work. (See pages 64–65 for spiraling.)

Step 2:
Add one round hydrangea head at the base of the foliage.

Step 3:
Add some more white ming fern.

Step 4:
When this is all in place, I begin to add height and interest with gypsophila stems. This also creates a softness and variety of texture. Tread these in, wiggling the stem as it goes into the desired space.

Step 5:
Next, add in lavender stems (be careful with these, since the buds can be quite fragile). I always add these in clusters, since the grouping is simple yet elegant. The lavender also makes your posy smell delightful, and the scent will last for a really long time.

Step 6:

Now all the material is in the posy. At this point, if any flowers have slipped, you can carefully move them up or around to create the shape you're aiming for. Foliage and flowers can easily slip position—the last step is when you neaten that up, rather than adjusting it as you go. It takes a little time to master this naughty wiggle; in fact, I usually don't fight with my flowers—they will end up where they want to go and often look better for doing so.

Step 7:

Time to tie off the posy. For a natural look, use simple garden twine. It's fitting and it completes the posy perfectly. Tying the posy is not just one string around the stems—I always wrap my string around twice, since this makes it much easier to keep the posy in place as you tie the bow.

Make sure you knot the string tightly, but not so tightly that you break it.

Step 8:

To tie the perfect bow, I have found the most visually appealing way is to tie it the opposite way of how we were taught to tie our shoes! Take your two loops or ears of twine and knot them in the middle. Cut the twine to any length you desire. And you have your cottage posy!

Step 9:

To finish, cut the stems to about one-third of the overall height of the posy.

8

6

9

7

ULTRAPOP POSY

Ultrapop posies are colorful and fun—they can be rainbows or gleaming with metallics. These posies are small and dainty, but the colors make them a bold statement. They are minimal in material, but they stand out. They are no shrinking violets!

I love being able to use color and paint in my designs, and luckily, dried flowers take paint like a piece of paper. Being able to create arrangements in any color adds enormously to its possibilities. I love the use of color to take a browned or dull flower to the next level—the color utterly transforms them!

Use much the same material as you would in a classic posy, with the crucial difference that all the flowers are painted. This arrangement is particularly striking, but any palette can be used; it really depends on the intended result. These bold colors will light up any space.

Commercially, these ultrapop posies are often used as gifts, upon the release of a particular collection of clothing or launch of a new product. I tailor the colors to go with any branding or complement the prominent colors of a collection of new-season clothing. Additionally, in winter months with gray skies above, ultrapop posies can brighten up a home, providing something to contrast those dark skies and lighten the mood.

MATERIALS
- **3–4 painted stems of flowers and foliage.** I used painted eucalyptus, hydrangea, and craspedia (billy buttons).
- **sharp scissors**
- **a bow to match your painted colors**

Step 1:
Start with the foliage stems; these make the bones of the arrangement and create a solid structure to build on.

Step 2:
Take the painted hydrangea (or whichever flower you have painted) and place it in the middle of the foliage; let it snuggle around it.

Add shorter cut stems of foliage at the front of the posy if it's looking a little flat or 2-D.

Step 3:
Add in height, using any painted flowers that work with your arrangement. I like to cluster these together to create the greatest impact and interest.

Step 4:
Tie off your posy. Sometimes I find it much easier to tie with twine first, so that nothing moves while you ready your complementary ribbon.

Step 5:
Cut the twine down so that it is just holding the posy in place. Get your chosen ribbon and loop it around the stems, covering the twine, and tie a beautiful bow.

Step 6:
Trim the stems to one-third of the size of the posy; this also makes the finished result neater.

COTTAGE-IKE POSY

This combination pairs a classic cottage posy with sculptural ikebana-style stems, a mix of two floral styles that together add dimension and perfectly harmonized contrast. Blending these two styles creates a modern spin on a traditional posy and becomes a new style in its own right.

I love being creative, not limiting myself to strict rules of floristry. I am always looking for and creating new methods of making my work. This style is no different. The more innovative, the better. As a maker, it's important to not become stagnant with your designs. Enjoy the process of thinking up a new or modern twist on the traditional.

This new style creates more of a sculpture than an arrangement. I have used bright strawflowers to contrast the soft browns and creams. The yellow billy buttons tie everything together. The result is visually different and interesting.

Such arrangements look beautiful sitting on someone's coffee table, on their bookshelf, or simply placed in a space that needs a little something extra. A bathroom, perhaps, where it would contrast against the hard stone or a simple enameled surface. These really can go anywhere; it depends on personal preference. I keep one like this on my bedside table, in my simple and restrained bedroom.

MATERIALS
- **3–4 varieties of dried flowers and foliage.** I used pea grass, pampas grass, and craspedia (billy buttons), and flannel flower.
- **1–2 stems of prepped ikebana-style stems.** I used strawflowers and hydrangea florets.
- **sharp scissors**
- **twine**

Step 1:
Prepare some ikebana-inspired stems. Take a branch (taller than your other material) and carefully glue the flowers onto the branches: it always looks most effective if you copy nature. Try not to glue these in a rigidly spaced design; don't be afraid to have some flowers facing different directions, since this will create depth and interest.

Step 2:
Start with your base material: this can be foliage, although I have used a type of pampas grass. Create a structure, the scaffolding for your arrangement.

Step 3:
Add in the bulk of the stems to help frame your ikebana pieces.

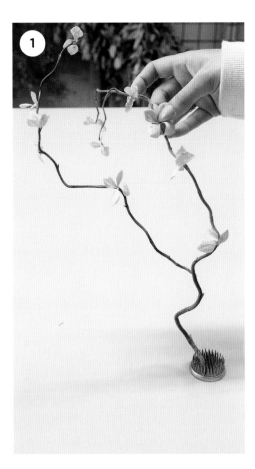

Step 4:
Now for the height: thread in the pea grass stems in clusters—this will add depth and interest to your posy.

Step 5:
Now it's time to add in the hero material—your ike stems. Add the taller stems to the back and the shorter ones to the front, spacing them out artistically.

Step 6:
Mend any of the flowers on your ike stems that may have gotten broken while making the posy.

Step 7:
Tie off using twine. You can also add a ribbon to match for added beauty, and cut your posy stems to length. Voilà!

STEP-BY-STEP
FLORAL PIECES

BOUQUETS

COTTAGE BOUQUET

Similar in style to a fresh bouquet, this traditional cottage version will last longer and give you more of a forever experience.

I love making these bouquets. I can use just about any dried flowers or foliage—obviously I have certain materials that I use most often, but the possibilities are endless. I really enjoy that these are an absolutely perfect present—a gift of flowers that will not be thrown out after a week.

For these more traditional bouquets, I particularly love using flowers and foliage that have a scent. I like to add eucalyptus or lavender, both of which I have in this recipe. The fact that these have a lasting scent is something that I really find unique. An added something special.

These bouquets work well in any space. They tend to be very neutral and therefore suit a wide variety of rooms. Most of my customers tell me that they have them on their dining-room table, while my retail clients have them on their store counters. Really, they can go anywhere; it's totally up to you.

MATERIALS
- **You'll need a lot of material here—the more the better!** I typically use about twenty stems depending on their thickness. This composition uses eucalyptus, nigella seed heads, limonium, and spike lavender.
- **sharp scissors and secateurs**
- **twine**

Step 1:
Start with your chosen foliage; the more the better. This naturally creates the foundations on which you will build your beautiful cottage bouquet.

Step 2:
One point I want to really emphasize here is that you shouldn't hold onto your bouquet with a viselike grip. Try to be confident enough to let your hand hold the bouquet loosely; it will help you in adding all your other bouquet components!

Start to thread in your larger flowers; this adds the bulk of the bouquet. Add them at different heights and levels, and don't forget the back of your bouquet!

Step 3:
Add in your clusters of flowers and try to spread them throughout your bouquet; this adds interest, and clusters always make even a traditional bouquet look more modern. And add a cluster at the back.

Step 4:
Turn your bouquet upside down so that you can see the back, and add material where it's needed. A cottage bouquet is typically viewed in full—in other words, all the way around.

Step 5:
The finishing touches! Add in the highlight material wherever it works best in your bouquet. Thread them in much like your other floral components. Do remember not to hold your bouquet too tightly; even if some of your flowers slip down, that can be adjusted later.

Step 6:
Keep turning your bouquet upside down, to check that every side has visually pleasing clusters of flowers.

Step 7:
Add in the traditional cottage flowers. I love using lavender for its scent but also for the variety of shape the flower gives the arrangement. Again, I thread these through and create taller and lower clusters throughout the bouquet.

Step 8:
Time to tie off! Twine is always appropriate in a cottage bouquet; the more natural the better!

Step 9:
Trim your stems to one-third the height of the bouquet.

IKE BOUQUET

Described in a nutshell, this style combines a traditional form of bouquet with ikebana elements. The bulk of flowers (or foliage, or both) contrasts with the minimal, sculptural form of the ikebana-styled stems. This creates an altogether modern take on a dried bouquet. I like to make these for my friends and family.

I particularly like this style because it combines so many of my practices. It is a style intentionally designed to be different from most other dried bouquets. Always changing and trying new techniques is especially important to a floral artist and designer. I never want to be stagnant in my designs or work, so I am forever conjuring up new ways to combine and create something completely different.

I have used materials in this bouquet that are new even to me. This is the first time, for example, that I have used ming fern— also called Sprenger's asparagus—a delicate South African native plant. See, even while I'm teaching you my recipes, I'm also learning myself! Hydrangea flowers are a floral I use often, especially, as here, pulled apart into individual florets and glued onto a stem.

I always have a new bouquet on our kitchen bench, relating to the colors in the house, or simply something I particularly like. They are usually made from unused bits and pieces to create a little something for myself and my husband to enjoy.

MATERIALS
- **4–5 different flowers and foliage.** I used dyed bunny's tail, limonium, and bleached ming fern (asparagus fern).
- **4–5 pre-made ikebana stems**
- **sharp scissors**
- **ribbon to complement your arrangement**

Step 1:
Take the bones of your arrangement (the material that is not ikebana based) and cross them together, while also creating a space in your bouquet in which to add your ike pieces later.

Step 2:
Add in your center base, which will frame your ike stems.

Step 3:
Thread in your whimsical stems (in my case, bunny's tail). I thread these in clusters to add greater definition and more interest.

Step 4:
Once the foundations of your bouquet are made, it's time to carefully incorporate the pre-made ike stems. These are to be threaded through the space that you created earlier. Keep these ike stems long and with space to breathe, because they are the hero pieces of your bouquet.

Step 5:
Adjust the heights of your ike pieces and also any flowers that have slipped down as you've been making the bouquet.

Step 6:
Tie off the bouquet with a suitable ribbon. I always prefer a big bow for this, a man-made contrast to your self-made bouquet. Also, I always cut my ribbons on an angle. It simply looks better and is less likely to fray.

Step 7:
Cut your bouquet to the desired length, using a sharp pair of secateurs.

ULTRAPOP BOUQUET

Ultrapop bouquets are, for the most part, all about the color, with a complementary but often-bold palette. Any flowers or foliage can have a new life of exciting hues and metallics. These arrangements would look utterly different if it were not for the lashings of color.

These are modern arrangements, made for fun and sheer color—and I love that they become quite the focal point in any room they occupy. The color is so dominant. There are no rules with ultrapop; just enjoy yourself and try new clashing or complementing colors together. Experiment! I particularly love using graffiti paint, meant for concrete walls, on my flowers for these modern arrangements.

These bouquets are perfect in a room as stand-alone pieces. Alternatively, the colors used to paint the flowers could be used to bring out a color theme in a space or mimic a company's branding. This is not a wallflower of an arrangement.

In this ultrapop bouquet, I've used deliberately contrasting material, since this helps the color appear quite different for each flower. A papery dried flower like these hydrangeas takes the color differently to a fluffy stem of phylicia. The texture of the whole arrangement becomes more obvious when painted.

The color really does change the natural look of the work.

MATERIALS
- **3–4 different types of dried flowers and foliage**
  I used (painted) hydrangeas, pea grass, and flannel flower (*phylica plumosa*).
- **ribbon to match your bouquet**
- **sharp scissors or secateurs**
- **spray paint**

Step 1:
Take the bones of your bouquet, the foliage—or in my case, my colored flannel flower—and crisscross it so that you create your base.

Step 2:
Thread in the large colored flowers to create a rounded but highly dimensional look. Cluster the flowers, adding different heights and levels.

Step 3:
Start threading through your softer, finer material in clusters throughout the bouquet. Don't forget the back. This clustering of flowers or foliage—especially if they are quite fine and delicate in appearance—makes for a multidimensional bouquet.

Step 4:
Add in any extra framing or foliage to surround, but not engulf, your blooms.

Step 5:
Tie off the bouquet with a suitable color ribbon—make it a complementary, bright, ultrapop color.

Step 6:
Trim your bouquet and enjoy it!

STEP-BY-STEP
FLORAL PIECES

IKEBANA STYLE

ULTRAPOP IKE

Ikebana-style arrangements change radically when using painted color. They tend to be much bolder; consequently I use the colors more sparingly, but the results are no less impressive. The structure remains much the same as other ikebana styles, but the color transforms the arrangement into a more dominant work, with the individual flowers more visually prominent.

Each and every ikebana-style arrangement is different. Adding ultrapop colors provides even more creativity. I live for creating; these arrangements fulfill that need of mine. The color possibilities are amazing, and I'm always trying new combinations of color and design.

I have used quite classic, familiar flowers in this arrangement: hydrangeas and nigella seed heads. When color is added, they become something entirely different. I love meddling with Mother Nature, so painting her hydrangeas gold is rather exciting. It's often quite hard to tell which flower it is once it's been painted, because paint changes its character: the natural appearance is altered—rightly or wrongly—but they are still beautiful. And bold.

These designs are more of a sculpture than an arrangement —I see them as floral works of art. They are perfect in a neutral room, where they become the focal point. Or on top of a café counter as something interesting to look at while sipping coffee or waiting for your order to arrive.

MATERIALS
- **3–4 painted, cut flowers and leaves.** I used nigella seed heads, manuka, and hydrangea florets.
- **3–4 types of painted stems/branches.** I used twisted willow and plum tree branches.
- **glue and a hot glue gun**
- **a kenzan** (flower frog)

Step 1:

Take your stems and arrange them any way you like, then push them into your kenzan. Make sure they are secure and will not move around as you are working.

Step 2:

Start by adding one of your flowers; I normally choose the largest or most-dominant ones—here I've used gold-painted hydrangea florets—followed by the foliage.

Step 3:
Add in the second "flower," actually a nigella seed pod, which I made the same color as the stem onto which I'm gluing it.

Step 4:
Add in the foliage, gluing and clustering the leaves as you go. I used manuka, which is very soft and fluffy, so sometimes glue more than one sprig on the same spot to add a little extra bulk as well as contrast and definition.

Step 5:
Check over your arrangement and assess the balance of the structure. Add any extra material if that balance is wrong.

IKE-ULTRAPOP NATURAL COMBO

This is a combination of ultrapop painted flowers and natural ikebana-style arrangement. It's a minimalist sculpture with a pop of color. Although it looks simple, this requires real attention to detail, since all the flowers are individually glued onto bare stems.

I love creating these ikebana-style arrangements, since they are always a detail-oriented challenge. For these pieces of art, patience is a must. Each glued flower or leaf position is consciously intended. These are not just glued at random but carefully considered. The finished result should be interesting to the eye and intriguing. Learning to trust yourself in the way you create space is a learned skill—the more space you have, the more your stems will stand out.

The materials I use in this recipe are chosen to contrast with one another—the soft bunny's tail against the ultrapop, pink, individual hydrangea florets, while the petite pink roses add a subtle natural brightness. The design is linear, so I am using long willow and straight stems as a base for my glued material. I deliberately choose to use less in these arrangements, since less is more with this style.

Because these works are essentially floral sculptures, they suit many places and spaces. They work equally well in private homes or public areas and are surprisingly versatile. Really endless. They suit so much.

MATERIALS
- **3–4 different types of natural flowers, plus one type of painted flower.** I used bunny's tail, petite roses, and painted pink hydrangeas.
- **2–3 different types of twigs.** I used corkscrew willow and wattle branches.
- **glue and a hot glue gun**
- **kenzan** (flower frog)
- **sharp scissors**

Step 1:
Make the branch base by securing the branches in the nails of your chosen kenzan. Try to make sure that these branches look natural, as if they have grown from the soil.

Step 2:
Start by adding one type of flower. I began with my petite roses. I kept them to one side and let them breathe.

Step 3:

Now for the natural bunny's tail. I always find with this type of ultra/ike combo that foraged material looks best and adds to its depth.

Step 4:

Now the final step: I add in my prepainted pink flowers (hydrangea florets). They don't even have to be perfectly painted; sometimes seeing the natural color come through is an unexpected bonus.

CLASSIC IKE-INSPIRED ARRANGEMENT

My ikebana-style arrangements are heavily influenced by the Japanese art. I have my own creative spin on these, but the fundamentals of design are much the same. An ike-style arrangement is simple and understated and respects the linear notions of traditional ikebana, but with dried flowers and foliage. Form is a huge factor in their design.

This style is an artistic challenge to create. What might look very simple is actually thoroughly thought out—that balance, that form, those hand-glued dried flowers and foliage— everything has been carefully considered. The intent is to make them so seamlessly that people still ask what plant it is. In fact, it isn't one plant, but many combined.

For this recipe I like to lean toward a neutral, natural palette, so I create these in muted, softer, calmer tones. I like these arrangements to merge with a client's space, not fight it. I want it to be peaceful, respecting the traditional art of ikebana. This style of ikebana-inspired work is most like a floral sculpture and therefore assumes the air of an art piece rather than a floral arrangement.

MATERIALS
- **3–4 types of flowers and foliage.** I used strawflower, jasmine buds, and eucalyptus leaves.
- **2–3 types of twigs.** I used twisted willow and blossom branches.
- **a kenzan** (flower frog)
- **glue and a hot glue gun**

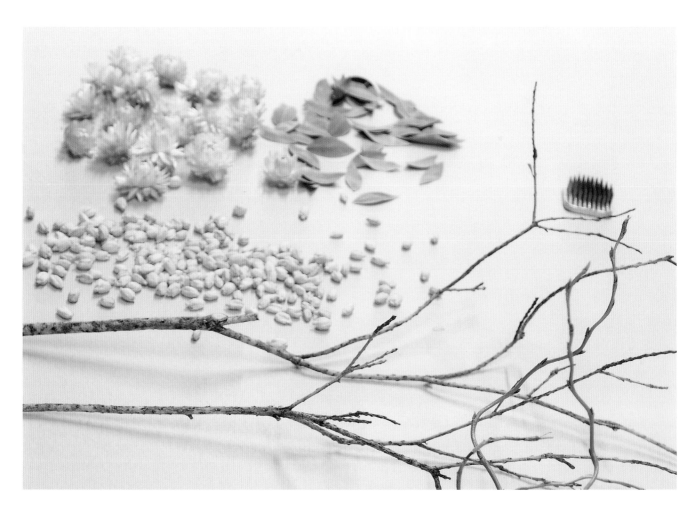

Step 1:

Choose your leaves. If they are not the shape you want, trim them to size.

Step 2:

Create your bare twig structure and secure them in your kenzan (frog). Sometimes the harder or thicker twigs need a small cut or slit at the base so that they easily go into the spiked nails of the base.

Step 3:

Start with gluing on your leaves. These tend to work most successfully on the most whimsical and twisted stems and make your arrangement look more natural.

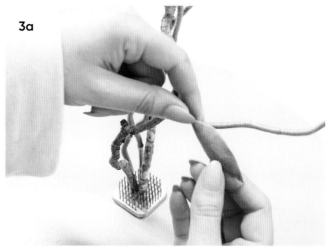

Step 4:

Add your hero flowers to the thicker stems. These strawflowers are mine, and since they are larger and more prominent, they suit a thicker stem.

Step 5:

Now add the smaller buds and cluster them. Dotting them around evenly does not provide the same visual appeal.

Finally, add any flowers or foliage where the arrangement might be lacking interest or form.

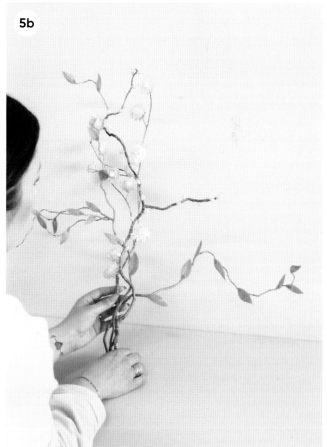

STEP-BY-STEP
FLORAL PIECES

WREATHS

MINIMAL WREATH

Minimal wreaths are more about the individual flowers and foliage. The design is intentionally simple. All the material used is understated but important. A minimal wreath is both sculptural, with a nod to the traditional, and elegantly understated.

These wreaths require a level of restraint that, like much in life, needs to be learned and practiced. Not overelaborating is the main drive. Learn to know when enough is enough.

I tend to use birch for all my wreaths. Its long slender branches are supple and easy to manipulate into a circular wreath shape—or a square, for that matter. The other material is provided by flowers and foliage that will stand out without fighting against each other. Furthermore, placement of this material is important. Don't use too much material. Keep simplicity in the back of your mind.

Wreaths like this have a multitude of uses. Because these are so understated, they can really go anywhere; they won't overpower a room.

MATERIALS
- **Long, soft twigs**—I used fresh birch because it's soft and malleable, with stems approximately 20 in. (1 m) long.
- **10–12 in. (20–30 cm) bowl, basket, or similar**
- **twine**
- **3–4 types of foliage and flowers.** I used jasmine buds, hydrangea florets, and eucalyptus leaves.
- **glue and a hot glue gun**
- **sharp scissors**

Making wreaths is a two-stage process, where the first stage is making the base and letting it dry, and the second stage is then covering it with all the beautiful foliage and florals. The steps to create the base are steps 1–5 in this project. For the other two wreath projects, I have assumed that you will have a pre-made wreath; if not, follow these first five steps to create one.

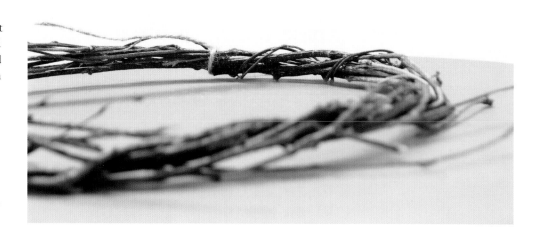

Step 1:
Starting with one stem, twist it into a circular shape approximately the size of the wreath you want to end up with.

Step 2:
Then, holding the first circular stem in one hand, pick up another and begin winding this loosely around the first, following the shape. Repeat this process, staggering the ends of each new stem around the circle until you have your desired wreath base thickness. Make this as thick or as fine as you like.

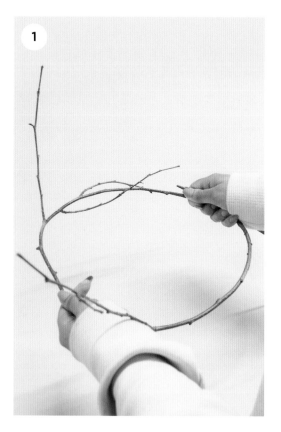

3

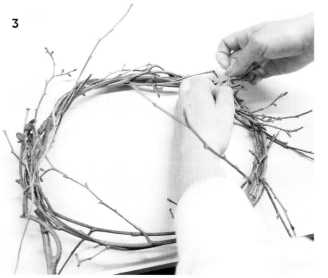

4

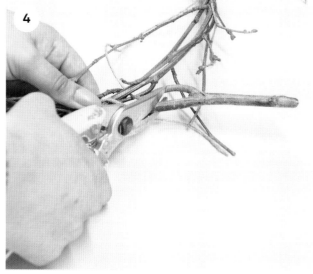

5

Step 3:
Using twine, cut several short lengths and tie them around the twisted stems at approximately four or five points around the circle. The twine will help secure the wreath base and help any cut ends stay in place.

Step 4:
Cut off any excess or protruding pieces of the twigs to finish the shape of your base.

Step 5:
Place the tied wreath on your shape holder and store the wreath for at least one week. This allows the twigs to dry and harden into the circle shape. Or, if you want the wreath to take on a natural form, lay it out flat, preferably in the sun or even in a warm linen closet if you have one.

Step 6:

When it's completely dry, take the wreath base and start to glue on the leaves. Only sparingly attach them—because this is a minimal wreath, the fewer the better.

Step 7:

Start to add in the flowers, but not too many.

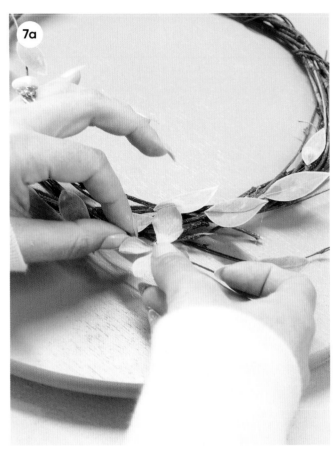

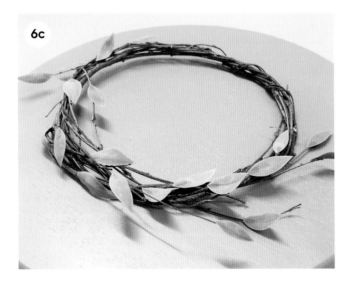

Step 8:
Add in the smaller, most delicate buds. I like to glue these to any sticking out twigs.

Step 9:
Check that all your gluing and flowers are neat but still looking natural and minimal. I cannot stress enough how important it is to keep this wreath simple.

COTTAGE WREATH

A cottage-style wreath is full of beauty through a combination of many floral materials. I like to make them so full you very rarely see the actual base. I layer and layer my material to create different depths, so there is always a visual point of interest all the way around.

This style leans toward the more traditional dried floral art of the past. Part of being a maker or an artist using dried florals is the history of techniques, many of which I can use in my own work.

I use a vast array of materials in cottage wreaths, and I tend to use the florals in this recipe the most. Hydrangeas are so versatile and are almost always used—you can rip them up to suit whatever size, and they come in loads of colors. I always use material that fits the job in mind, or materials that complement one another.

Many of my cottage wreaths hang in nurseries. The delicate softness in their style naturally lends nostalgia to a newborn's room and acts like a little artwork to commemorate and celebrate the birth. I always have one hung above my bed; perhaps we really do want these in our most nurturing and safe places—a totem of love and protection.

MATERIALS
- **6–7 different varieties and lots of it.** I used hydrangeas, lavender, strawflowers, eucalyptus, limonium, gypsophila, and nigella seed pods.
- **a pre-made wreath base**
- **glue and a hot glue gun**
- **sharp scissors**

Step 1:
Take your pre-made wreath base or make one following the instructions on pages 132–133. Start by gluing all your leaves all the way around the wreath.

Step 2:
Start to add in one of your bigger types of flower (strawflowers here) all around the wreath base, clustering them, and gluing them less rigidly, more whimsically. Since this is a natural-style wreath, we want natural to be the byword.

Step 3:
Add in your next-biggest flower or a certain special something you've chosen (I used nigella seed pods). Glue these around the wreath to create dynamic interest.

Step 4:
Take the hydrangea heads and cut them apart in uneven clusters of florets, then glue them randomly around the wreath.

Step 5:
Start gluing in your buds. I always use lavender because it gives such a beautiful scent as well as looking great.

Step 6:
Add in your fluffiest foliage or flowers (limonium and gypsophila), or both. Make them a bit longer so that they rise above the level of flowers already on the wreath.

Step 7:
Add in your last floral touches (limonium here). I often use material that contrasts with the rest of the flowers and foliage to create a natural "pop."

WREATH COMBO

These wreaths are a mix of cottage-style flowers combined with glued ikebana stems. They are visually pleasing and a satisfying combination of two popular floral designs. They are a perfect balance between the two styles: the best of both worlds.

Wreaths are not only for Christmas but for all year round—and that's how I approach them. Using ikebana stems also means I can get a lot more out of my material and create a more visually interesting piece. I love making these because I can use so many learned skills.

I like to use birch branches for my wreaths, so in this half wreath, I let the birch be seen. This plainness makes the rest of the wreath more interesting. Around the base, the cottage flowers and foliage are layered to create depth and a 3-D look. The ikebana stems burst out and add to those lines and levels.

I have a wreath hanging above my bed. Other people hang them around their houses—I know of one that decorates a hallway. They really can be hung anywhere you want a special something.

MATERIALS
- **1–2 types of fluffy foliage.** I used two colors of smoke bush.
- **2 types of dried florals, one (or more) with berries and small leafed foliage.** I used hydrangeas, jasmine buds, viburnum berries, and bugleweed.
- **sculptural twigs.** I used twisted willow stems.
- **a pre-made wreath base**
- **glue and a hot glue gun**
- **sharp scissors**

Step 1:

Take your pre-made wreath base and glue on clumps of hydrangeas, pulled apart into small clusters—not the whole flower, just parts of it. Create a nonuniform pattern; don't be too precious here, feel free to just glue the clusters randomly. This wreath is informal and natural.

Step 2:

Add your fluffy foliage into the gaps, at different heights and levels.

Step 3:

Add different-colored foliage—I used leaves from a red smoke bush.

Step 4:

Start gluing in your twigs (mine are willow) horizontally across the wreath for your ike elements.

5a

6

5b

7

Step 5:
Now you have your twig base for the ike elements. These will stand out from the cottage base and be a highlight. Add your small buds first (preferably ones that contrast in color); these are jasmine buds.

Step 6:
Add in the berries. I chose vibernum berries because they vary so much in color, from dark purple to soft reds to green.

Step 7:
Glue small leaves onto your unadorned twigs.

Step 8:
Make sure every twig has been covered, and the overall appearance of your ike/cottage wreath is your reward.

8

STEP-BY-STEP
FLORAL PIECES

CIRCLETS

HALF CIRCLET

Half hair circlets are easy and charming to wear and can go over or under any hairstyle. They are popular for celebrations, especially weddings and engagement parties. Many people wear them to festivals, music or otherwise. Colors are less restrained in the latter, when color and fun are most important.

A half floral crown, my favorite to make, is delicate yet durable, and surprisingly robust. If they are damaged during festivities, they can quickly be mended or modified!

With half floral crowns, I really can use any plant material. Here I've run with colorful flowers to show that the compostional possibilities are endless. I have chosen brighter, more fun colors, as a contrast to the restrained cream palate of a bridal crown. I bind the wires with raw silk and loop the ends so that a ribbon of silk can be tightened to the wearer, the perfect fit, so it will not fall off!

Most floral crowns are for brides or bridesmaids; however, some people just love to wear flowers in their hair. I know I do!

MATERIALS

- **6–7 different varieties of dried flowers, plus one type of leaf (cut and prepped).** I used petite roses, statice, two different colors of larkspur, limonium, and bleached pink eucalyptus.
- **floristry wire (the thicker the better)**
- **ribbon (in a contrasting color).** I used white silk ribbon.
- **glue and a hot glue gun**
- **sharp scissors**

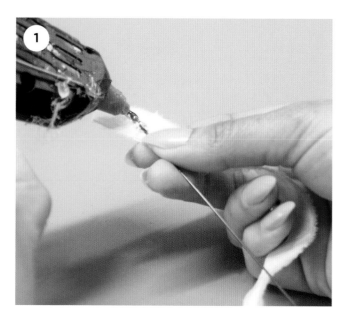

Step 1:
Begin with the wire and glue the ribbon at the top to secure it.

Step 2:
Start wrapping the ribbon: then snip off any ribbon at the top of the wire. Wrap ribbon all the way to the end, keeping it as tight as possible so that the ribbon does not slip and you don't have to use glue throughout.

Step 3:
Once you are at the end of wrapping your ribbon, glue it off and cut it as you did at the start. Then snip off any excess ribbon.

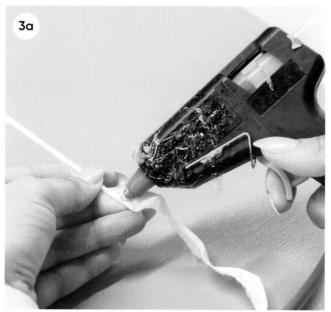

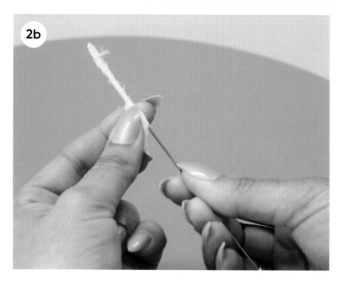

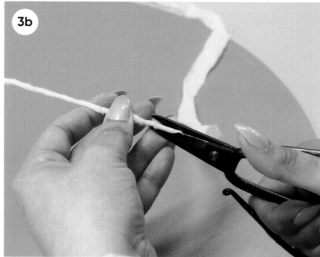

Step 4:
Once you have your ribbon-covered wire, gently bend it into a half circle. Then, at each end of the wire, twist it to create two loops through which the rest of your ribbon will be threaded.

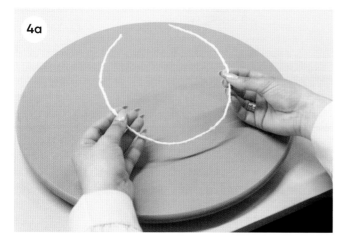

Step 5:
With the circlet base made, secure the circlet upright, with whatever you have at your disposal (I used my flower kenzans).

Step 6:
Start to glue your base material: I usually create a base of leaves before I add any flowers—this trick also makes it look neatest from the underside and hides any wayward gluing.

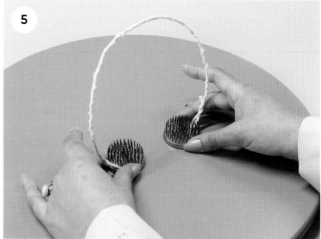

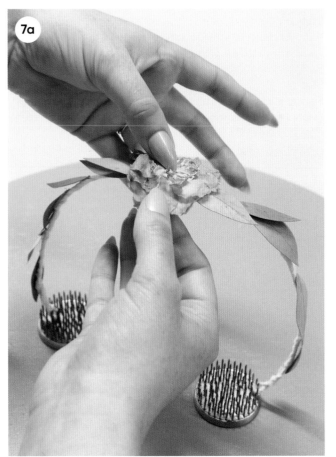

Step 7:
When your leaf base is secure and glued, it's time to add in your flowers. Here I've used larkspur. I tend to put my hero flowers at the front first, then work around the base. Let some flowers sit under the leaves. This creates depth and makes your circlet look more natural, rather than strict and too perfect.

Step 8:
Add in your other larger flowers, nestling them in among the first layer of flowers.

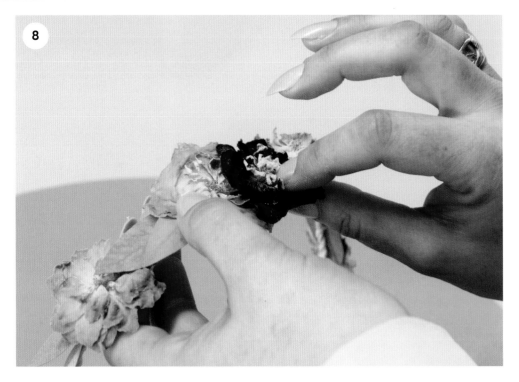

Step 9:
Add in your texture, your fluffy flowers or foliage. I've used limonium and statice.

Step 10:
Add in some of your smaller flowers, clustering them to create interest or using them to hide any unwanted dabs of glue.

Step 11:
Once all your flowers and foliage are glued in and you are happy with how your flower circlet looks, thread your remaining ribbon through the holes at the ends (which you made earlier). Cut the ribbon, keeping as much length as possible and remembering that the lucky lady who wears this will likely tie it on with a bow.

FULL CIRCLET

Made full circle, this is the most opulent of floral hair circlets, which can be worn on top of the head like a crown or lower like a headband. These circlets are delicate and beautiful to wear. Because they use dried flowers, they can be worn for more than one occasion. They are most effective when made in soft hues and delicately bound, adding to the dedication to beauty.

This full circlet has the color palate of soft creams and whites—traditional bridal colors. Floristry wire is bound by ribbon; every element is considered for the perfect crown.

Obviously, floral crowns denote a certain celebratory element for their use. Most of mine are worn by brides or for special occasions when crowns are appropriate. One beauty of these

is that they can be kept forever, a keepsake of a special time or day, or even hung as a floral wreath after they have been worn. But they do not finish there; they are often treasured and kept for years.

MATERIALS

- **3–4 different types of flower.** I used strawflowers, ming fern (asparagus fern), gypsophila, and statice.
- **floristry wire** (two lengths of sturdy thickness to go around the head with length to spare)
- **ribbon to match your floral colors**
- **sharp scissors/secateurs**
- **glue and a hot glue gun**

Step 1:
Take two wires about the circumference of a head, then cross and twist them together, as neatly as possible.

Step 2:
Start to bend the wire into a circular shape, taking into consideration that this is going to be worn on someone's head. I always use my own head to assess how big the circlet needs to be. Then cross and twist the wires together, creating a looped circlet.

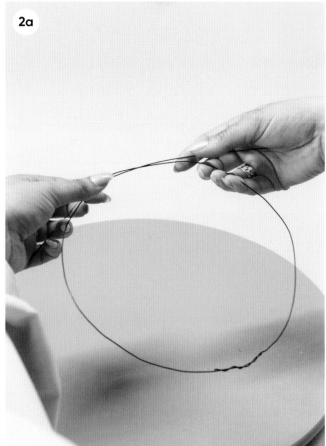

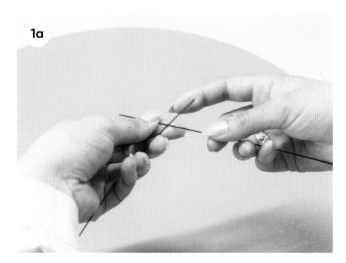

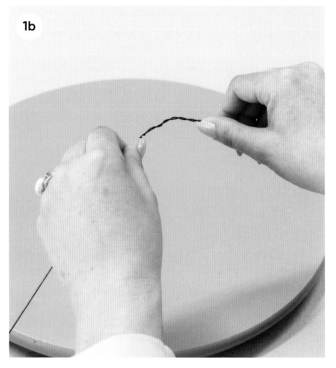

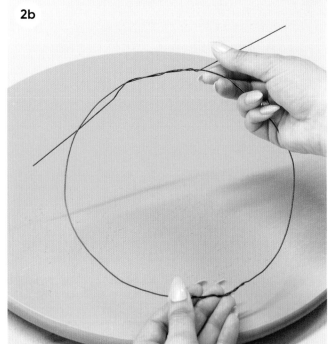

Step 3:
Use the scissors/secateurs to cut off the excess wire.

Step 4:
At one point, glue your ribbon into place.

Step 5:
Start wrapping the ribbon tightly around your wire frame; if you do this tightly, you won't have to use glue all the way through the binding.

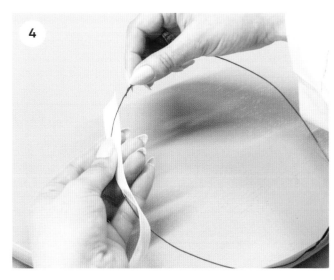

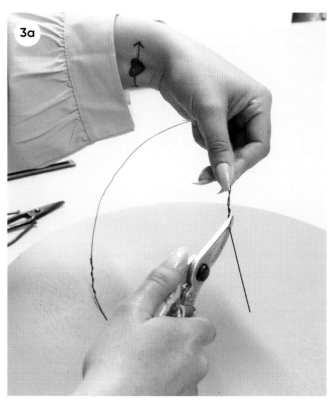

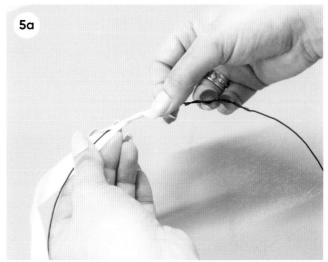

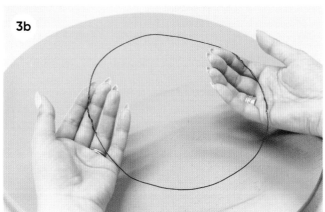

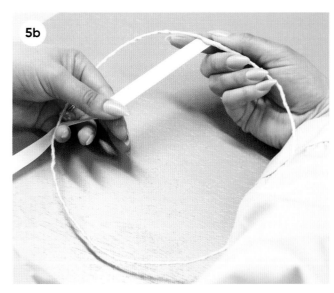

Step 6:

When the wire is completely covered and wrapped in ribbon, glue the remaining end to the wire, as neatly as you possibly can. Snip off any remaining ribbon and glue the end down into place. The circlet base is now ready for flowers.

Step 7:

Start with your biggest flowers, adding them around the entirety of the circlet base. This time I have used strawflowers.

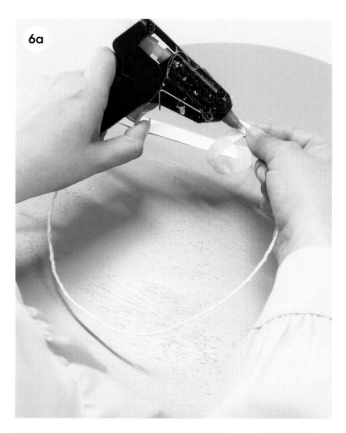

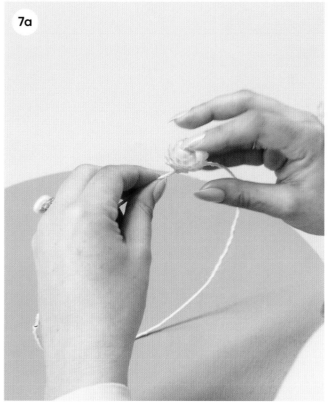

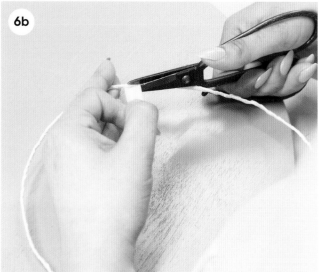

Step 8:

Glue in all the other flowers you have. I like to keep this quite loose and free, so that the circlet does not look too regular and has different points of interest. This is especially important with a full circlet.

Step 9:

Add in any extra flowers to areas that might be lacking or need just a little more love. And then you are finished—well, you've finished making—now you must put that crown on some lucky person's head!

NATURAL CIRCLET/HALF COVERING

Natural circlets are made entirely from flowers and foliage, including stems from nature for the base. The base is a perfect shape for a circlet, with all the flowers at the front to sit on top of the head. The base is not uncomfortable to wear. Birch is light and it keeps its shape.

Working with a birch base means there is no need for ribbons and wire. Natural circlets are unique in that respect. I enjoy making them because using everything from nature is less wasteful and kinder to the earth. They can even be composted—but no one throws these away.

The flowers I use differ with each circlet, although this one uses the most popular—roses, gypsophila, and hydrangeas. These are materials I use most often; they are all quite study and robust flowers, and that is needed in a hair circlet. Naturally, wearing any kind of dried flowers creates more

movement and thus inevitable damage. So, I always use material that I think will be most robust for the wearer—while it's still beautiful. Natural floral crowns are used much the same as any other hair circlets. Celebration is perhaps their main purpose—whatever that celebration may be! These are often kept, framed or hung as a reminder of that special celebration.

MATERIALS

- **3–4 different types of flowers, plus 1 type of neat foliage.** I used hydrangea florets, gypsophila, jasmine buds, and spray roses, plus wattle tree leaves.
- **a pre-made circlet base.** I used a birch for the base (this is made in exactly the same way as the wreath base on pages 132–133).
- **glue and a hot glue gun**
- **a simple stand to keep the circlet upright.** I used a brown cardboard base, with pins to keep it in place.

Step 1:

Secure your circlet in place so you can work on it.

Step 2:

Start by gluing on clusters of foliage as naturally as possible, but only to the top half of the circlet. Use different sizes and forms of leaves.

Step 3:

Once you have a base of foliage and flowers on your circlet, you can start adding in your hero flowers such as these rosebuds.

Step 4:
Add in your smaller, more petite buds (jasmine), clustering them as you go.

Step 5:
Add in your "fluffy" flowers, such as gypsophila, to supply texture and richness to the circlet; also add any extra leaves you may have to frame the hero flowers.

Step 6:
Add any extra layers to your circlet if there are gaps; otherwise you are done!

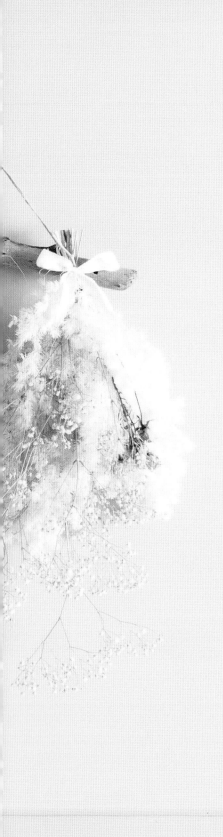

STEP-BY-STEP
FLORAL PIECES

HANGING
PIECES

FLORAL FOAM-BASED WALL HANGING

These wall hangings are art—they are hung up and are meant to be looked at. They are often larger in scale. I can make them any size and have made some so large they did not fit out of my studio door! These hanging arrangements are hungry for material. I use many flowers and foliage; in fact, the more the better. These huge wall hangings use more traditional floristry skills than usually used with dried florals. They are a real challenge, but absolutely worth the effort.

For this design I used material that is largely soft and light; the smoke bush and the pink ming fern (asparagus fern) are like clouds. The deep-red roses contrast with this cloud and create a focal point that leads your eye diagonally. The whole is framed with bare willow stems. I use floral foam sparingly and always

use eco floral foam. However, since these are made to last, I do not have the nagging guilt of floral foam going into a landfill. Such pieces are for a special wall. Most of mine are bought to decorate softer rooms, such as bedrooms or nurseries. There is something about the cloud of flowers that seems peaceful and therefore naturally lands in spaces that are calm.

MATERIALS
- **4–5 types of fluffy foliage or flowers (or both).** I used two types of smoke bush and ming fern (asparagus fern).
- **sculptural short twig lengths.** I used twisted willow stems.
- **floral foam / Dry Oasis ®**
- **sharp scissors**
- **sharp knife or craft knife**

Step 1:

Cut your dry floral foam (or Oasis ®) into a rounded shape. If you leave it square, your hanging won't look natural, plus you'll have to cover more foam with more material.

Step 2:

Start to add in a single kind of foliage (this time, smoke bush). I always work asymmetrically, since I find this creates a better finished result. Add different lengths to create depth.

Step 3:

Now add a different but similar material, even using the leaves to create texture. Leave a gap in the foam for your hero flowers or foliage.

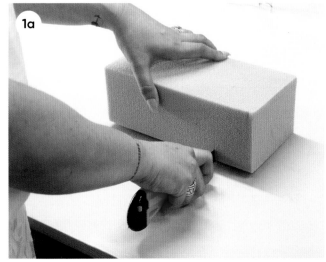

Step 4:
Find gaps in the foam and start to add your contrasting foliage.

Step 5:
Fix in your hero flowers, clustering them at an angle in the center of the arrangement, with different heights and levels.

Step 6:
Use any extra material to hide any spots where you can still see the foam. If you have covered it completely and thoroughly, you don't need to do this, but it always pays to check every angle of your work to make sure the foam is invisible to the naked eye.

Step 7:
Add in the bare sculptural twigs to highlight your hero flowers and to give the wall piece more structure and appeal.

HANGING DRIFTWOOD ARRANGEMENT

I love to experiment with different materials. Because we live near the coast, driftwood is easy to find, and I can't stop myself trying to incorporate its wave-softened beauty into my work. I like to have the driftwood showing, not hidden; it is so unique—every branch is different.

It is important to be inspired by what you can collect in your own area, wherever that maybe. Exploring your surroundings leads directly to that inspiration. Collecting driftwood, flowers, foliage—foraging—is one of my favorite things to do. And gathering driftwood is a perfect example of respecting your surroundings. There is nothing more pleasurable than making things with what you find.

Driftwood makes a perfect hanging branch for floral arrangements and is very different from the more usually used branches, in its soft, curved, washed, and sun-bleached condition. Driftwood is a delight to decorate with florals. I like to use arrangements that are soft in nature, since the bleached-out colors and softer hues really harmonize with driftwood.

MATERIALS

- **2 types of whimsical, fluffy flowers and foliage, plus 3 long flower stems.** I used gypsophila, ming fern (asparagus fern), and spray roses.
- **a suitable length of driftwood**—or if you don't live near the coast, a branch is a perfect substitute.
- **glue and a hot glue gun**
- **ribbon**
- **twine**

Step 1:

Gather your material into two equal amounts, as if you were making bunches of flowers.

Step 2:

Start to create your bunches of flowers or foliage, remembering that this will be hung on the wall, so the back is not seen and therefore not important.

Step 3:

Once you have your bunch ready, tie it off using long lengths of twine. Wrap it tightly several times, to a depth of about 0.5 in. (1 cm). Remember to keep your two long lengths of twine, then knot your binding to the back of the bunch.

Repeat this process for the second bunch—they don't have to be identical. I typically don't make exact copies with these; I let some flowers sit higher or lower to create greater interest and depth.

Step 4:

Trim the bunch stems to length; the less stem the better, since we want the florals to be the highlight.

Step 5:
Once you have your two bunches, it's time to tie them to the driftwood (or branch). Tie your twine tightly to the back of the driftwood, and don't forget to keep your lengths of twine. Add a little dab of glue for extra strength.

Step 6:
When the bunches are securely tied and glued (to the back), it's time to make your hanging lengths. This is where that extra length of twine comes in. Tie the twine to create a triangular formation, knot it, and cut it as close to the tie as possible. Finally, add a dab of glue to the back of the knot to keep it strong, so it will not come undone.

Step 7:
Now create two bows to match the colors in the arrangement. These should then be glued over the top of the visible twine at the front of the hanging.

IKEBANA-STYLE HANGING

These installations are more worthy of the term "art" than any of the other works. They are made to hang on a specific wall, so every part of the making and material should be closely considered.

This style of work often takes on its own shape and form. I have in my mind the general size and shape, but as I work with a base of wired and glued stems or branches, these hanging arrangements often take on a direction of their own. That's what I love most about them—I let these arrangements do their own thing.

I use a mixture of branches and stems as the base of these installations; the thickest in the middle, with laterals added to create depth and dimension. I mix the florals and foliage, layering and gluing with the intention that not only do the floral materials have to hide the structural wires and glue, they also have to create interest. Using different materials in these larger

pieces makes sure that that depth and interest are always clear to the person viewing the final arrangement.

Such pieces are hung in homes, retail spaces, and hotels. Some people even lay them flat on a dining-room table and use them as a centerpiece. They are versatile enough to use in many different ways and for many different purposes.

MATERIALS
- **5–6 types of different flowers and foliage.** I used larkspur, several different-colored hydrangea heads, jasmine buds, and eucalyptus leaves.
- **2 different types of twig in various lengths and in great quantity.** I used twisted willow and deleafed rata (a New Zealand native) branches.
- **floristry wire**
- **glue and a hot glue gun**
- **sharp scissors**

Step 1:

Create the twig base—the foundation into which your flowers will be glued. I try to keep mine angular and not too spidery: it's very easy to make a structure that looks like the biggest spider you could possibly see, only covered in flowers!

Make sure you use a lot of glue and wire around the glued points. Keep all this tight and don't worry if you can see the green wires, since they will be covered with flowers and foliage in the next steps.

Step 2:

Once you have made your sturdy twig base, start to add in all the other twigs—but don't let the structure become too flat; we want this to be 3-D. Don't be afraid to add twigs of different heights and levels.

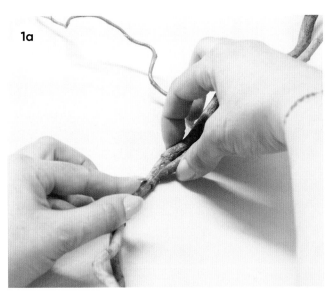

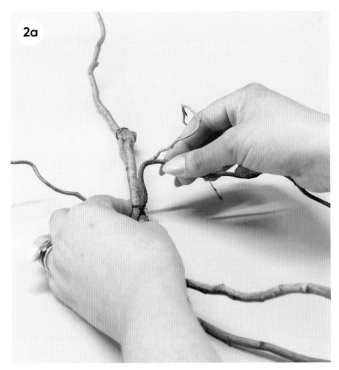

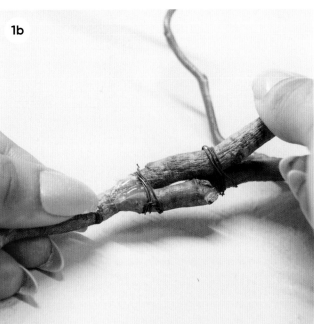

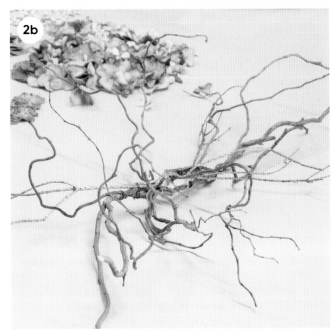

Step 3:
Add in your largest, flattest flowers (here, nice blue larkspur), trying to glue them over the wires but also not creating something too neat and structured.

Step 4:
Add in the leaves asymmetrically, to hide the glue and wiring that may still be visible.

Step 5:
Begin adding in other flowers onto the remaining twigs, staggering them and spacing them unevenly.

Step 6:
When all your larger flowers and foliage have been incorporated, add in the smaller, more petite buds—such as jasmine—to create contrast.

As a pioneer in the dried-floral revival, Antonia De Vere has created a body of work spanning styles from delicately restrained, sculptural, fully hand-trimmed and hand-assembled ikebana inspired pieces to super contemporary colored, full, and textural ultrapop pieces. Working with commercial clients throughout New Zealand, Antonia designs florals across a vast spectrum of scales. From tiny vase-based stems to huge suspended installations, her works can be seen in many of the country's top eateries, vineyards, and boutiques.